W9-AWG-235

CORE INFLATION

OTTO ECKSTEIN

Harvard University
Data Resources, Inc.

Prentice-Hall, Inc., Englewood Cliffs, New Jersey 07632

Library of Congress Cataloging in Publication Data

Eckstein, Otto.
Core inflation.

Bibliography; p.
Includes index.
1. Inflation (Finance)–United States.
I. Title
HG540.E25 332.4'1'0973 81-8485
ISBN 0-13-172643-9 AACR2
ISBN 0-13-172635-8 (pbk.)

This book originated in a study prepared for the Joint Economic Committee, U.S. Congress, *Tax Policy and Core Inflation,* and in earlier testimony for the Committee's Study of Economic Change. I am grateful to Robin Siegel for exceptionally capable research aid, to Frank Cooper for running the model simulations, and to Lyn Hadden for producing the manuscript.

Editorial/production supervision by Steven Young
Jacket design by Carol Zawislak
Cover design by Edsal Enterprises
Manufacturing buyer: Ed O'Dougherty

Printed in the United States of America

10 9 8 7 6 5 4 3 2 1

Prentice-Hall International, Inc., *London*
Prentice-Hall of Australia Pty. Limited, *Sydney*
Prentice-Hall of Canada, Ltd., *Toronto*
Prentice-Hall of India Private Limited, *New Delhi*
Prentice-Hall of Japan, Inc., *Tokyo*
Prentice-Hall of Southeast Asia Pte. Ltd., *Singapore*
Whitehall Books Limited, *Wellington, New Zealand*

CONTENTS

PREFACE

Why have rising unemployment and worsening inflation gone hand in hand in recent years? Why has the underlying inflation rate kept rising? Why have the periods of relief from inflation been so brief?

This book offers a theory to explain these puzzling phenomena. The central concept is "core inflation," defined as the trend rate of increase of the price of aggregate supply. All supply can be traced back to labor and capital, the two primary factors of production. Labor costs are determined by the rate of wage increase adjusted for the productivity trend. Capital costs are set by interest rates, equity prices and the relative price of capital goods. While there are numerous short-lived inflationary elements in the economy, the underlying thrust comes from the gradual rise in the price of labor and capital, the core inflation rate.

The temporary inflation forces are classified into two headings: "shock inflation," such as increases of oil and food prices, and "demand inflation," the classic pull of tight labor and product markets on the price level. Total inflation is the sum of all three sources: core, shock and demand.

The core inflation theory is designed to measure the benefits of supply-side policies on the price level. Tax policies to stimulate capital formation, labor supply and productivity directly lower the core inflation rate by acting on capital and labor costs.

The theory stands as a counterpoint to the rational expectations hypothesis which is currently receiving much attention. Core inflation is persistent because wages and long-term interest rates are based on stubbornly held price expectations of workers and investors. If expectations could be improved dramatically by changes in economic policy, core inflation would melt quickly. But will the public believe in such policies and react positively? This issue, perhaps the most important in economics today, is examined empirically. The conclusion here is one of inflation pessimism. The U.S. postwar record points to persistent price expectations rather than easy persuasion.

This book originated in the study *Tax Policy and Core Inflation* prepared for the Joint Economic Committee, U.S. Congress, and earlier testimony presented to the Committee's Study of Economic Change. I am grateful to Robin Siegel for exceptionally capable research aid, to Frank Cooper for conducting the econometric model simulations, and to Lyn Hadden for producing the manuscript.

Otto Eckstein

CHAPTER 1

INTRODUCTION AND SUMMARY

Inflation has been building up for 15 years and has brought the economy to a very difficult juncture. With no choices left, the government was forced to create a severe recession in early 1980 in a desperate attempt to escape permanent double-digit inflation. Yet, even while suffering the recession, everyone recognized that it offered no solution to the inflation problem, just temporary relief that would quickly disappear in a recovery.

If there ever was a time when inflation was not viewed as a serious problem, it is long gone. Today inflation is associated with declining real purchasing power of workers and businesses, and with the loss of the productivity trend which has lifted the United States economy for over a century. U.S. exports are losing their share of world markets and foreign goods are displacing our own at home.

This volume presents a new theoretical and quantitative analysis of the inflation process. It decomposes the inflation into (1) the classic demand factor, (2) shocks such as food, energy, and micro policies, and (3) the core component which has gradually become deeply embedded in the cost trends for labor and capital.

The analysis shows how we have reached the present condition. Long periods of excess demand raised the core inflation rate to 4% during the Vietnam War. Food and energy shocks added several more points in the mid-1970s. New shocks and more excess demand drove the core inflation rate to more than 8% during 1979 and is moving it toward 10% in 1980. The brief intervals of relief created by the recessions and good food prices fooled monetary and fiscal policymakers into a sense of improvement when, beneath the surface, core inflation kept getting worse. It also shows how the world energy situation has contributed to the development of core inflation and casts a long, dark shadow over future prospects.

Is there a way out of the deteriorating inflation picture? This study uses the 800-equation DRI macro model in tandem with a new Core Inflation Model to explore the possible benefits of more cautious monetary and fiscal policies

Chart 1.1
Core, Shock, and Demand Inflation
(Year-over-year percent change, SA)

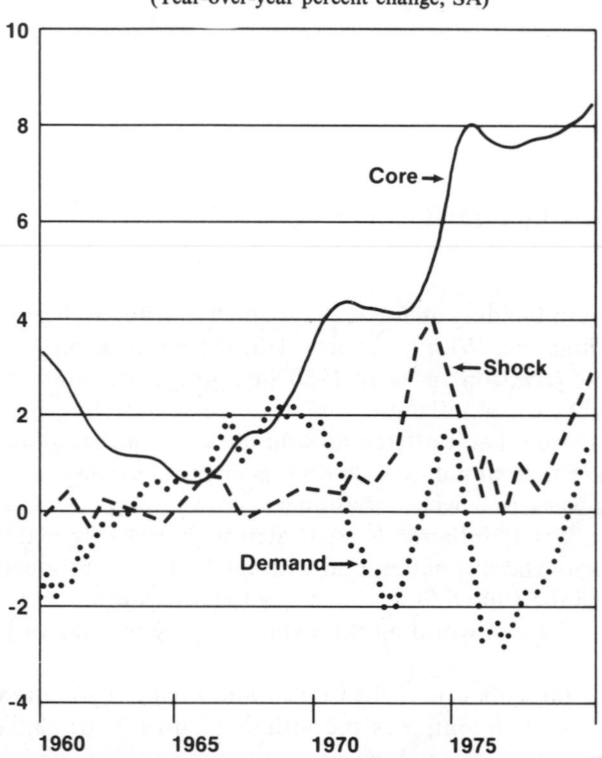

and major new tax policies to provide stronger incentives for business capital formation.

The principal conclusions of the study are these:

(1) The prospect for core inflation is not good. With productivity lagging and wages likely to accelerate in response to 1979-80's double-digit inflation results, unit labor costs will be advancing very rapidly. Capital costs also will continue high and rising, now that long-term interest rates more fully reflect the inflation record and the cost of equity capital is pushed up by the poor stock market performance. If the United States does not change its approach to economic policy, there is every reason to believe that core inflation will continue to become worse.

(2) Shocks will continue to be an important source of inflation. The current round of OPEC price increases and the impending boosts in Social Security tax rates will create a shock inflation rate averaging 2% over the next three

Table 1.1
Core, Shock, and Demand Inflation
(Average annual rates of change)

	1960 to 1965	1965 to 1970	1970 to 1973	1973 to 1979
Unit Labor Cost Trend *(weight .65)*	2.2	2.0	4.0	6.6
"Equilibrium" Wage Gains	4.2	4.8	5.8	7.8
Actual Wage Gains	3.1	5.8	6.6	7.9
Price Expectations	1.8	2.3	3.8	6.0
Unemployment Rate (level)	5.5	4.0	5.3	6.5
Productivity Trend	2.0	2.7	1.7	1.1
Actual Productivity Gains	3.1	1.4	2.8	0.5
+ ***Capital Cost Trend*** *(weight .35)*	0.4	2.4	4.9	8.6
Actual Rental Price of Capital	-0.2	5.9	4.6	11.3
Prime Rate (level)	4.56	6.32	6.72	8.87
New High-Grade Corporate Bond Rate (level)	4.42	6.40	7.67	8.68
Price Expectations	1.7	2.5	4.1	6.2
= ***Core Inflation Rate***	1.5	2.0	4.2	7.1
Shock Inflation Rate	0.0	0.3	1.2	1.8
WPI—Farm Products	0.2	2.4	16.7	5.4
WPI—Fuels	0.0	2.2	8.1	20.4
Trade-Weighted Exchange Rate	0.6	-0.8	-5.0	-0.3
Social Security Tax Rate (difference)	0.002	0.003	0.006	0.004
Minimum Wage ($/hour)	1.147	1.445	1.600	2.245
Demand Inflation Rate	-0.3	1.5	-0.5	-0.7
Capacity Utilization in Manufacturing (level)	0.829	0.867	0.822	0.823
Unemployment Rate (level)	5.5	4.0	5.3	6.5
Consumer Price Index	1.3	4.3	4.6	8.5

years. Under DRI's (perhaps sanguine) assumption of future OPEC price increases at a real rate of 4%, with domestic energy being gradually deregulated and with other shocks likely to make at least a small contribution, the probable shock rate of the early 1980s is near 2% and will average over 1% for the decade even if our luck improves. This continuing push from shocks makes it difficult to achieve a permanent downturn in the core inflation rate through the traditional methods.

(3) Careful monetary and fiscal policies are a prerequisite for any approach to inflation control. In order to stabilize the core inflation rate near an 8% plateau in the first half of the 1980s, demand management would have to aim at an unemployment rate of 8% following the 1980-81 recession. To bring the core inflation rate down significantly through fiscal and monetary policies

alone would require a prolonged period of deep recession, bordering on depression, with the average unemployment rate held above 10%. This is clearly not a feasible approach to the problem.

(4) To achieve better progress on inflation, it is necessary to turn to the supply side of policy. Table 1.2 summarizes the simulation results of adopting a sizable package of tax incentive programs to liberalize both the investment tax credit and depreciation allowances. The investment tax credit is assumed to be boosted by 2.7 points. The depreciation change is a four-year reduction in the economic lives of equipment. The revenue effect of this package is $15.7 billion in the year of adoption, growing to $32 billion by 1990. The tax incentives are financed through reduced government spending. Highlights of the effects of this simulation are:

- Real business fixed investment is up by 9.8% by 1985 and 15.6% by 1990, raising the capital stock by 3.4% by 1985 and 7.2% by 1990.
- The enlarged supply of capital boosts potential GNP by 1.1% by 1985, and elevates the growth rate of potential by 0.2 percentage points per year for the entire decade.

Table 1.2
Reducing Core Inflation Through Investment Tax Credits and Liberalized Depreciation
(Difference from baseline path)

	1980	1981	1982	1983	1984	1985	1990
Policy	Difference in Level						
Average Tax Lifetime (years) of Producers Durable Equipment	-4.0	-4.0	-4.0	-4.0	-4.0	-4.0	-4.0
Investment Tax Credit (rate)	0.027	0.027	0.027	0.027	0.027	0.027	0.027
Corporate Profit Tax Accruals (% difference)	-15.7	-15.4	-17.9	-24.1	-24.7	-22.3	-32.7
Macroeconomic Effects	Percent Difference in Levels						
Real GNP	0.1	0.3	0.3	0.2	0.7	1.2	3.7
Total Consumption	0.1	0.3	0.2	0.0	0.4	0.7	2.1
Nonresidential Fixed Investment	0.4	5.7	8.5	7.0	7.5	9.8	15.6
Investment in Residential Structures	1.2	5.6	1.5	-4.5	0.0	4.6	9.9
Net Exports	1.5	1.0	5.2	11.3	11.6	14.1	35.7
Government Purchases	-0.3	-3.7	-4.8	-2.9	-3.3	-4.3	-2.9
Capital Stock	0.0	0.7	1.6	2.2	2.7	3.4	7.2
Long-Run Supply	Percent Difference in Levels						
Potential GNP	0.0	0.0	0.2	0.5	0.8	1.1	2.6
Inflation and Unemployment	Difference in Percent Rate of Change						
Core Inflation	-0.2	-0.7	-0.7	-0.8	-1.0	-1.0	-1.3
	Percent Difference in Levels						
Consumer Price Index	-0.1	-0.3	-0.4	-0.6	-1.0	-1.4	-4.0
Average Hourly Earnings	0.0	0.0	-0.1	-0.2	-0.4	-0.7	-2.2
Real Wages	0.1	0.2	0.3	0.4	0.6	0.9	2.3
Unemployment Rate (difference in level)	0.0	-0.1	-0.1	0.1	0.1	0.0	-0.4
Capacity Utilization (difference in level)	-0.010	-0.013	-0.017	-0.032	-0.030	-0.027	-0.053

• The improved capital-labor ratio adds a similar 0.2 points per year to the rate of productivity growth.

• Real wages are up an extra 0.9% by 1985, helping to produce a 0.7% increase in real consumption. Housing activity is diminished slightly over this period because the increased level of business capital formation crowds out some mortgage supplies.

• The reduction in the core inflation rate is 1.0 percentage point in 1985, and 1.3 points by the closing years of the decade.

(5) While a full point reduction of the core inflation rate would be a major achievement and would firmly put the economy on a path of improvement as compared to its present unfortunate trajectory, the policies are clearly insufficient to bring the inflation rate down to acceptable levels. To make further progress, other avenues of policy must be explored. The shocks from

Chart 1.2
The Core Inflation Rate and
the Consumer Price Index
(Year-over-year percent change, SA)

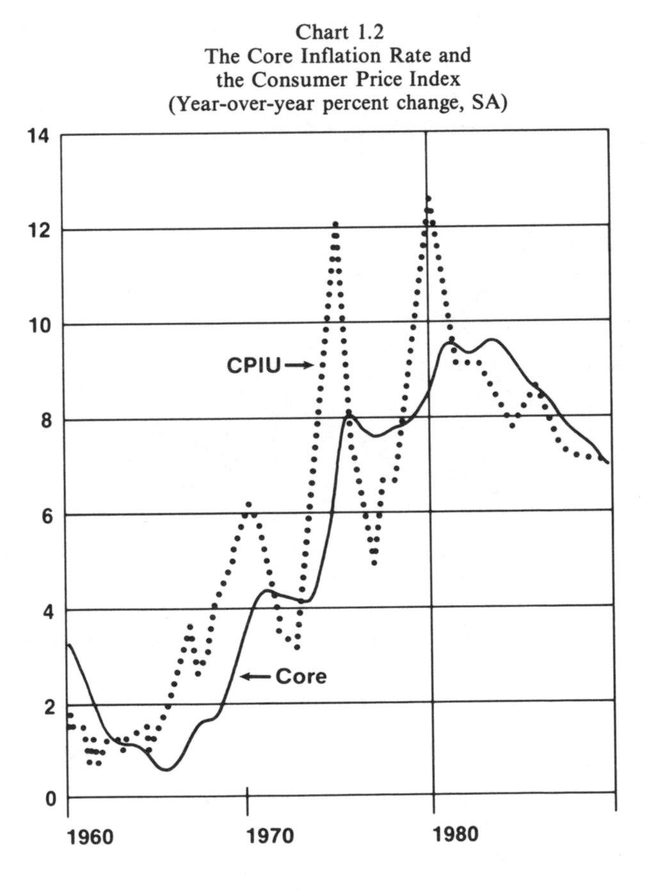

energy must be reduced by cutting oil use and boosting domestic supplies. They also include a renewed effort to build up the stock of technical and scientific knowledge through investment in research and development, changes in the personal tax burden which may augment the supply of labor at least to a small degree and encourage productivity, and measures to enlarge the total supply of capital to the economy through increased personal saving. Measures that would reduce the unemployment rate of disadvantaged groups also would help in the struggle against inflation both by adding to the effective labor supply and by making it acceptable to manage aggregate demand in a more cautious fashion.

CHAPTER 2

THEORY OF CORE INFLATION

Inflation has proved to be the most stubborn problem confronting economists. It has proved impossible to forecast with acceptable accuracy or to devise effective cures. This chapter advances a theory to decompose inflation into its main causes. The next chapter expresses it as a fully quantified econometric model. Succeeding chapters apply the new method to the historical record, analyze the role of energy, and quantify policy choices to reduce the inflation rate.

1. Core, Demand, and Shock Inflation

The aggregate inflation rate has proved volatile and dominated by "surprises." Variations in aggregate demand have long been known to affect the price level, yet other factors have frequently obscured this relationship. Such shocks as energy and food price explosions or government micro policies of regulation and taxation have been seen as alternative theories of inflation. A suitable conceptual structure must bring the several inflation mechanisms together into a coherent, logical theory.

A satisfactory theory of the inflationary process must make room for three kinds of effects. First, the state of demand affects short-term price behavior. Second, shocks, i.e., sudden changes in particular costs, can add to the short-term inflation rate. Third, the succession of short-term demand and shock effects produces a core inflation rate which has a great propensity to persist.

The core rate is the trend increase of the cost of the factors of production. It originates in the long-term expectations of inflation in the minds of households and businesses, in the contractual arrangements which sustain the wage-price momentum, and in the tax system. Core inflation can be made better or worse by the particular circumstances of any short period, but it can only be modified gradually because no brief experience will undo the cumulative effects of previous reality.

The conceptual structure can be set out as follows. Let the total inflation rate of a period be equal to the sum of the three separate inflation sources: core, demand, and shock.

$$(1)\ \dot{p} = \dot{p}_c + \dot{p}_d + \dot{p}_s,$$

where p is the inflation rate, $\dot{p}_c$ is the core rate, $\dot{p}_d$ is the demand rate, and $\dot{p}_s$ is the shock rate.

The core rate of inflation can be viewed as the rate that would occur on the economy's long-term growth path, provided the path were free of shocks, and the state of demand were neutral in the sense that markets were in long-run equilibrium. The core rate reflects those price increases made necessary by increases in the trend costs of the inputs to production. The cost increases, in turn, are largely a function of underlying price expectations. These expectations are the result of previous experience, which, in turn, is created by the history of demand and shock inflation. In a competitive, Cobb-Douglas economy with Hicks-neutral technological change, the long-term equilibrium price, p_c, can be written as,[1]

$$(2)\ p_c = Aq^{a_1}w^{a_2}e^{-ht},$$

where q is the rental price of the capital required per unit of output, w is the wage rate of the unit labor requirement, h is the aggregate factor productivity rate of technological progress, and a_1 and a_2 are the Cobb-Douglas factor share weights which, under the assumption of constant returns to scale, must sum to unity.

The core inflation rate is the change in the long-term equilibrium price along the balanced growth path. It can be written

$$(3)\ \dot{p}_c = a_1\dot{q} + a_2\dot{w} - h.$$

[1]For a fuller theoretical treatment of equilibrium price in this particular macro context, see William D. Nordhaus, "Recent Developments in Price Dynamics," in Otto Eckstein, ed., *The Econometrics of Price Determination* (Federal Reserve Board, 1972), pp. 28-30; and James Tobin, "The Wage-Price Mechanism: Overview of the Conference," *ibid.*, pp. 5-7. Nordhaus shows the equilibrium price results under various production functions besides the standard Cobb-Douglas case.

Robert J. Gordon's analysis also uses the Nordhaus formulation as the basis for developing a core price equation, defining it as a general price equation incorporating demand and cost factors. See his "The Impact of Aggregate Demand on Prices," Brookings Economic Papers, 1975:3, pp. 613-662. For a more recent use of his approach, see Jon Frye and Robert J. Gordon, "The Variance and Acceleration of Inflation in the 1970's: Alternative Explanatory Models and Methods," NBER Working Paper No. 551, September 1980.

Modigliani and Papademos have developed a price equation emphasizing persistence of expectations, exogenous prices, and demand. See Franco Modigliani and Lucas Papademos, "Targets for Monetary Policy in the Coming Year," Brookings Economic Papers, 1975:1, pp. 141-163.

The present formulation of the core inflation rate as the trend of the aggregate supply price is designed to permit analysis of the forces on the supply side: productivity, capital formation, tax policy, etc., and to provide an analytical framework which can absorb the various sources of inflation in a detailed theoretical and quantitative manner.

The rental price of capital depends on the relative price of capital goods, depreciation and tax parameters, and the financial cost of capital. Let

$$(4)\ \dot{q} = \alpha(r, J_q),$$

where r is the composite cost of financial capital and J_q is the composite tax variable on capital and its income. Financial cost is determined by the long-term inflation expectations embodied in nominal interest rates and equity yields, so that

$$(5)\ \dot{q} = \alpha(\dot{p}^e_q, J_q).$$

Similarly, wages on the equilibrium path are determined by the price expectations underlying wage claims and possible tax effects J_w, or

$$(6)\ \dot{w} = \beta(\dot{p}^e_w, J_w).$$

Therefore, the core rate of inflation depends on long-term price expectations in labor and capital markets, tax provisions, and factor productivity, i.e.,

$$(7)\ \dot{p}_c = a_1\alpha(\dot{p}^e_q, J_q) + a_2\beta(\dot{p}^e_w, J_w) - h.$$

Price expectations are formed on the basis of inflation experience, as measured by distributed lags on actual prices, and need not be the same for bond buyers as for workers. Thus,

$$(8)\ \dot{p}_c = a_1\ \alpha((\Sigma_{t=0}^{-\infty}\ \lambda_t\dot{p}_t), J_q) + a_2\ \beta((\Sigma_{t=0}^{-\infty}\ \mu_t\ \dot{p}_t), J_w) - h.$$

Since the actual inflation of a period, t, is composed of the three components,

$$(9)\ \dot{p}_t = \dot{p}_{c_t} + \dot{p}_{d_t} + \dot{p}_{s_t},$$

and the core inflation rate is affected by the actual record of inflation as processed into current expectations, the core inflation rate can be written in terms of previous demand and shock inflation, productivity, and taxes,

$$(10)\ \dot{p}_{c_t} = \delta(\dot{p}_{d_t}, \dot{p}_{d_{t-1}} \ldots, \dot{p}_{s_t}, \dot{p}_{s_{t-1}} \ldots, h_t, h_{t-1} \ldots, J_{q_t}, J_{q_{t-1}} \ldots, J_{w_t}, J_{w_{t-1}} \ldots).$$

The demand inflation rate will depend on utilization rates of resources derived from the level of aggregate demand and factor supplies. Presumably both the unemployment rate and the operating rate of physical capital are pertinent, and the effects are nonlinear. Thus,

$$(11)\ \dot{p}_d = \gamma(u_l, u_{cap}).$$

The shock inflation rate is, by definition, exogenous to the analysis. While, in fact, such shocks as OPEC and food prices are in part endogenous with aggregate demand playing the conventional price-lifting role, they are considered here to be determined primarily by noncontrollable conditions: OPEC political-economic decisions in one case, weather and crop conditions in the other. Government shocks, such as payroll taxes, are exogenous because they are considered to be policy levers.

Core inflation can be expressed, then, in terms of the previous history of aggregate demand, shocks, and productivity, where the latter two factors are mainly expressions of supply-side phenomena and exogenous cost shifts. Thus,

$$(12)\ \dot{p}_{c_t} = f(u_{l_t}, u_{l_{t-1}}, \ldots, u_{cap_t}, u_{cap_{t-1}}, \ldots, \dot{p}_{s_t}, \dot{p}_{s_{t-1}}, \ldots, h_t, h_{t-1}, \ldots, J_{q_t}, J_{q_{t-1}}, \ldots, J_{w_t}, J_{w_{t-1}}, \ldots).$$

2. Shocks and the Noninflationary Unemployment Rate

The conceptual structure of equations (1-12) can be used to analyze various macro relationships, but the extensive lag structure hides significant analytical conclusions. A two-period simplification allows these conclusions to emerge.

Suppose the two periods are the present, t_o, and the past, t_{-1}. Also, suppose price expectations are formed in the same way by the suppliers of labor and capital, and the tax effects are excluded. Also, suppose utilization in labor and physical capital markets is the same and measured by u. As before,

$$(13)\ \dot{p}_o = \dot{p}_{c_o} + \dot{p}_{d_o} + \dot{p}_{s_o}.$$

The core inflation rate is formed from the expectations process,

$$(14)\ \dot{p}_{c_o} = \alpha\dot{p}^e{}_o = \alpha\beta\dot{p}_{-1}.$$

The coefficient α subsumes the expectation of factor suppliers for positive real gains which may or may not be offset by actual factor productivity gains. The coefficient β is a measure of the completeness of the learning process in the formation of price expectations. Then,

$$(15)\ \dot{p}_o = \alpha\beta\dot{p}_{-1} + \dot{p}_{d_o} + \dot{p}_{s_o},$$

and

$$(16)\ \dot{p}_o/\dot{p}_{-1} = \alpha\beta + \dot{p}_{d_o}/\dot{p}_{-1} + \dot{p}_{s_o}/\dot{p}_{-1}.$$

Suppose $\dot{p}_{d_o} = 0$ and $\dot{p}_{s_o} = 0$, i.e., demand is at its equilibrium level and there are no shocks. Then,

$$(17)\ \dot{p}_o/\dot{p}_{-1} = \alpha\beta.$$

Under a unit elasticity of expectations which would be rational along the equilibrium path,

$$(18)\quad \alpha\beta = 1, \text{ so } \dot{p}_o = \dot{p}_{-1},$$

or the inflation rate remains unchanged and price expectations are fulfilled. Suppose

$$(19)\quad \dot{p}_d = \gamma(u^* - u),$$

where u^* is the natural rate of unemployment based on friction, search, and incentive phenomena in the labor market. Then,

$$(20)\quad \dot{p}_o/\dot{p}_{-1} = \alpha\beta + \gamma(u^* - u)/\dot{p}_{-1} + \dot{p}_{s_o}/\dot{p}_{-1}.$$

In order to leave the inflation rate unchanged, i.e., $\dot{p}_o/\dot{p}_{-1} = 1$, with $\alpha\beta = 1$,

$$(21)\quad \gamma(u^* - u) = -\dot{p}_{s_o}.$$

If the function is linear and homogeneous, (21) becomes

$$(21a)\quad u^{**} = \dot{p}_{s_o}/\gamma + u^*,$$

where u^{**} is the noninflationary unemployment rate, the rate which avoids acceleration.[2]

3. *The Noninflationary and the Natural Unemployment Rates*

The distinction between u^*, the natural unemployment rate, and u^{**}, the noninflationary unemployment rate, is fundamental: u^* is the rate at which the level of demand does not add to inflation. It is derived from the organization of the labor and product markets, the demographic situation, search phenomena, the nature of tax and transfer incentives, and other supply considerations. If unemployment is at the natural rate but there are shocks, the actual inflation rate will exceed the core rate and gradually worsen it. If inflation is not to become worse in the presence of shocks, unemployment must exceed the natural rate to serve as an offset, i.e., $u^{**} > u^*$.

[2]Many writers have used the terms "natural" and "noninflationary" unemployment rate interchangeably. The distinction is drawn here to indicate the rate created by the interaction of the economy's structure with the level of demand as a rate which is lower than the rate required to avoid inflation once exogenous shocks enter the situation. For a good example of the definition and measurement of the natural unemployment rate, see Jeffrey M. Perloff and Michael L. Wachter, "A Production Function-Nonaccelerating Inflation Approach to Potential Output: Is Measured Potential Output Too High?" in Karl Brunner and Allan H. Meltzer, eds., *Three Aspects of Policy and Policy Making: Knowledge, Data and Institutions,* Carnegie-Rochester Conference Series, 10, 1979.

The current structure of the economy, following nearly a decade of underinvestment, creates one other distinction: the natural rate of unemployment is not associated with equilibrium in total factor use. Thus, when the labor market is in equilibrium at u^*_l, the capital market is in disequilibrium, or $u_k > u^*_k$, and there is demand inflation originating in an excessively high rate of utilization of physical capacity.

4. Tracing the Sources of the Inflation Process

The various inflation components must be pursued further to their root causes. The productivity trend in the core inflation rate is partly determined by the rate of capital formation, human resource investment, and technological progress. The resource utilization rates depend on private spending propensities and fiscal and monetary policies which determine aggregate demand. A theory of investment is needed for capital supply, a theory of labor-force participation for labor supply.

To trace fully the three components of inflation to their causes requires a full description of the economy such as is represented in a complete macroeconomic model. As will be seen in the discussion of the empirical treatment in the next chapter, the Core Inflation Model is drawn almost entirely out of the 800-equation DRI Quarterly Econometric Model of the U.S. Economy. Thus, there is no need to develop a special purpose theoretical or empirical model to conduct a full core inflation analysis.[3]

Apart from the particular decomposition of the problem into its three components to provide analytical focus, the core model makes strong empirical statements only in one crucial regard: the formation of price expectations for determining long-run capital and labor costs is a gradual learning process rather than a quick response to policies or other particular events. The theory is consistent with a weak form of the rational expectations viewpoint that price expectations are free of bias in the long run, but it is inconsistent with the stronger viewpoint that these price expectations are formed quickly from particular policy announcements, exogenous events, or movements in such variables as the money supply or actual prices observed over a short time.

[3]The core inflation analysis can also be treated as a stand-alone analytical device in which its inputs—the level of aggregate demand, the shock rate, the rental price of capital, the rates of wage and productivity increase—are treated as exogenous.

CHAPTER 3

CORE INFLATION: ECONOMETRIC MODEL

The empirical execution of the core inflation analysis consists of two tasks: (1) development of a small model defining and relating the concepts of the core inflation analysis, and (2) the development of the DRI model to represent more fully the critical supply effects that help determine potential output and productivity. The formal links between the two models are summarized in Chart 3.1.

In this study, inflation is equated with movements in the consumer price index, the index considered by the public to be the indicator of inflation. This index currently suffers from an upward bias due to its treatment of homeownership costs. To make sure that the analysis does not depend on the choice of index, it was tested on the deflator for consumer expenditures and found to be little changed.

1. Measuring the Core Inflation

The core inflation rate, or the trend in the aggregate supply price, is the weighted average of the trend rates of increase of the rental price of capital and unit labor cost. Chart 3.2 shows the historical record of the rental price of capital and of its trend. The raw series is quite volatile, principally because of the short-term variations in interest rates and stock yields created by financial conditions, monetary policy, and various other short-term market factors. The trend rate is calculated as a Pascal lag with a decay factor of 0.15. This smoothed series is a more appropriate measure of capital costs because of the extended lag structure for investment, corporate financing, and pricing.

The macro model's long-term interest rate equation underlying the rental price of capital has price expectations as one of its main determinants. This term is calculated through a Pascal lag on the implicit price deflator for personal consumption. Its Pascal lag has a decay factor of 0.79 for a mean lag of 7.5 quarters. The coefficient on prices is not statistically different from

Chart 3.1
DRI Quarterly Econometric Model of the U.S. Economy:
Core Inflation Model

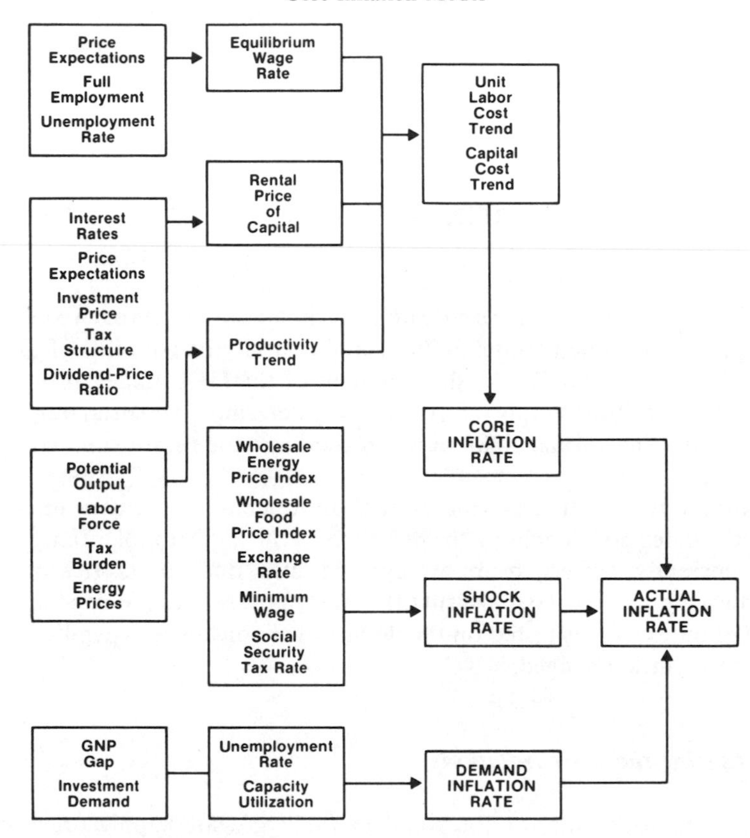

unity, indicating that interest rates are consistent with a weak rational expectations hypothesis of unbiased expectations with a slow learning process. Other terms in the interest rate equation represent the yields in competing capital markets including stocks and mortgages, the volume of new bond issues, and the supply of bank reserves as an indication of the economy's liquidity and of monetary policy. The interest rate equation, along with the other equations discussed in this chapter, is shown in Chapters 9 and 10.

The wage component of unit labor costs is measured by the Bureau of Labor Statistics' hourly earnings index which is adjusted for overtime and industrial mix. Hourly earnings rather than total compensation are used because payroll taxes, which account for much of the difference between the two series, are included in the "shocks" created by government policies.

Chart 3.2
The Rental Price of Capital
(Year-over-year percent change, SA)

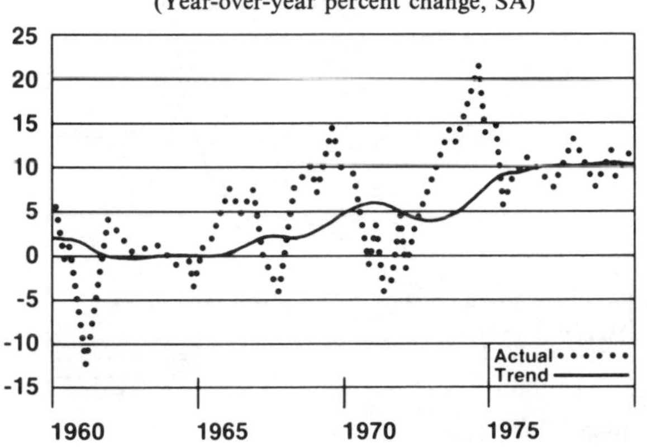

The wage equation in the macro model contains two price expectations terms: the first is the rate of consumer price increase of the preceding four quarters, which reflects the impact of near-term inflation on wages through cost-of-living escalators and the more sensitive wages of unorganized workers; the second is a long-term price expectations factor based on a Pascal lag with a decay factor of 0.85, or a mean lag of 11.3 quarters. Of the two price expectations terms, the long-term variable has the larger weight. They sum to near unity, indicating that wages too are consistent with a rational expectations hypothesis, one in which short-term price changes are discounted to be partly nonrecurring and perhaps reversible, but long-term price behavior is fully reflected in wages.

Because wages are affected by short-term labor market demand conditions, the definition of the core wage rate requires correction for unemployment. The demand effect is removed by evaluating the wage term for each quarter as if unemployment were at its equilibrium level (defined historically as the Council of Economic Advisers' full-employment unemployment rate), using the coefficient on unemployment in the wage equation. Thus, core labor costs are based on equilibrium-employment wage changes. Chart 3.3 compares actual wage gains to the equilibrium trend.

Wages are corrected by the labor productivity trend to derive the unit labor cost component of core inflation. Productivity is estimated in the macro model as a function of potential productivity (potential output relative to full employment labor supply) adjusted for cyclical variation in utilization levels. The productivity equation also includes terms to capture the effects of the tax burden and the relative price of energy. The productivity trend is derived by

Chart 3.3
Average Hourly Earnings
(Year-over-year percent change, SA)

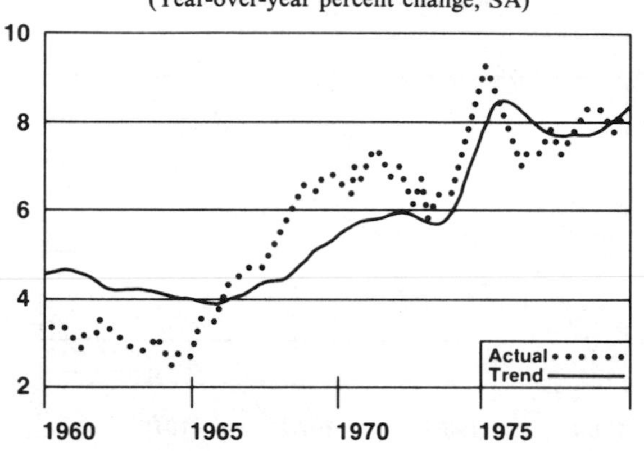

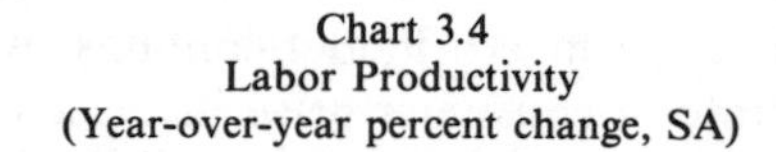
Chart 3.4
Labor Productivity
(Year-over-year percent change, SA)

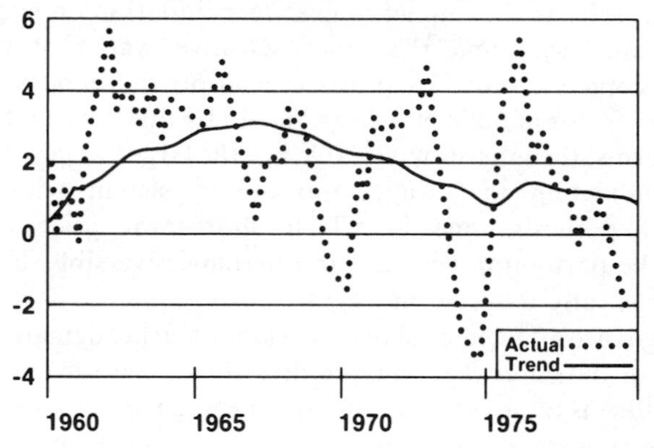

setting the cycle variables at their equilibrium levels and smoothing the resulting series with a Pascal lag with a decay factor of 0.79 (see Chart 3.4). The relative weights attached to labor and capital are derived from the extended Cobb-Douglas production function in the model, yielding coefficients of 0.65 on labor and 0.35 on capital.[1]

[1]Use of a pure Cobb-Douglas approach as sketched in equation (3) calls for total factor productivity rather than labor productivity, or else the use of shifting weights. For expositional clarity and to allow use of variables in the DRI macro model, labor productivity was used here.

. Chart 3.5
The Unit Labor Cost Trend:
Wage Trend — Productivity Trend
= Unit Labor Cost Trend
(Year-over-year percent change, SA)

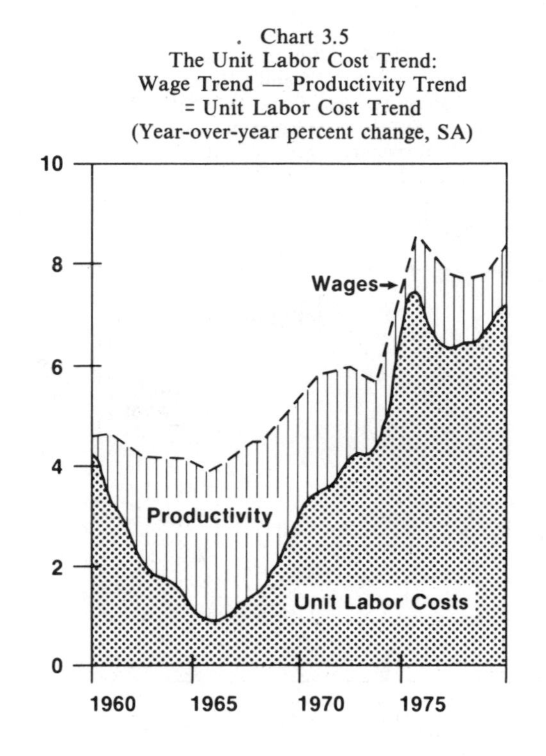

2. *The Shock Inflation Rate*

It is beyond the current state of empirical economics to model fully the various shocks to the price level which originate with government and other exogenous forces. They include, in principle, any shift in the aggregate supply function. Only those elements that are already represented in the DRI model have been used in the empirical definition of the shock variable. This list contains energy and agricultural prices, the exchange rate of the dollar, payroll taxes, and the minimum wage. Government regulation was not modelled at this stage, because there are no indices of regulation of sufficient accuracy to allow a serious econometric analysis.

In order to isolate the components of the shock variable, full model simulations were run to measure reduced-form impacts on the price level. The relationships identified through the model runs yield time series which are combined with historical values for the exogenous variables to derive the shock effects. Chart 3.7 shows the historical record of such an exercise. Equations (22-26) represent the "reduced form" estimates drawn from the

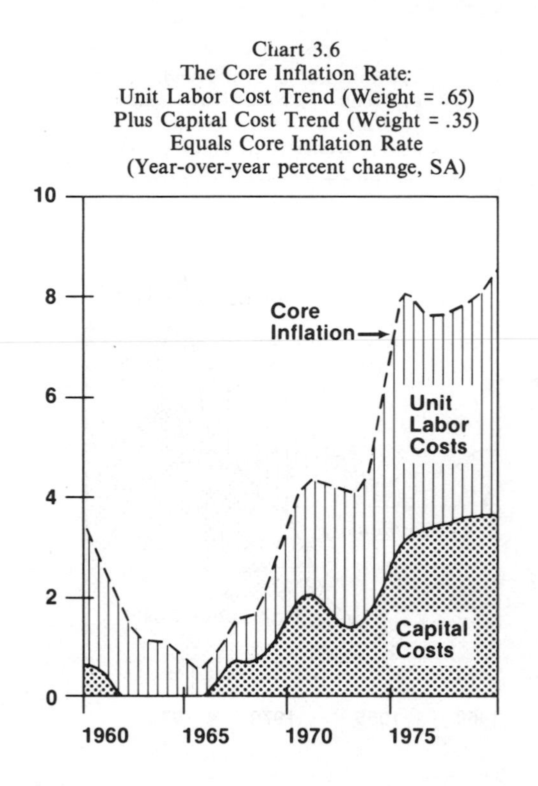

Chart 3.6
The Core Inflation Rate:
Unit Labor Cost Trend (Weight = .65)
Plus Capital Cost Trend (Weight = .35)
Equals Core Inflation Rate
(Year-over-year percent change, SA)

model simulations. The relationships linking the energy, agriculture, and exchange rate changes to the consumer price index are

$$(22)\ \dot{p}_{s_{WPI05}} = .008*\Delta WPI05 + .013*\Delta WPI05_{-1} + .014*\Delta WPI05_{-2} + .015*\Delta WPI05_{-3}$$

$$(23)\ \dot{p}_{s_{WPI01}} = .007*\Delta WPI01 + .012*\Delta WPI01_{-1} + .014*\Delta WPI01_{-2} + .014*\Delta WPI01_{-3}$$

and

$$(24)\ \dot{p}_{s_{EXCH}} = -.001*\Delta EXCH - .003*\Delta EXCH_{-1} - .005*\Delta EXCH_{-2} - .008*\Delta EXCH_{-3}$$

where *WPI05* is the wholesale price index for fuels, related products, and power, *WPI01* is the wholesale price index for farm products, and *EXCH* is the Morgan Guaranty Trust trade-weighted index of the exchange rate for the U.S. dollar. The effects of payroll taxes and minimum wages are modelled as follows,

Chart 3.7
The Shock Contribution to Inflation
(Year-over-year percent change, SA)

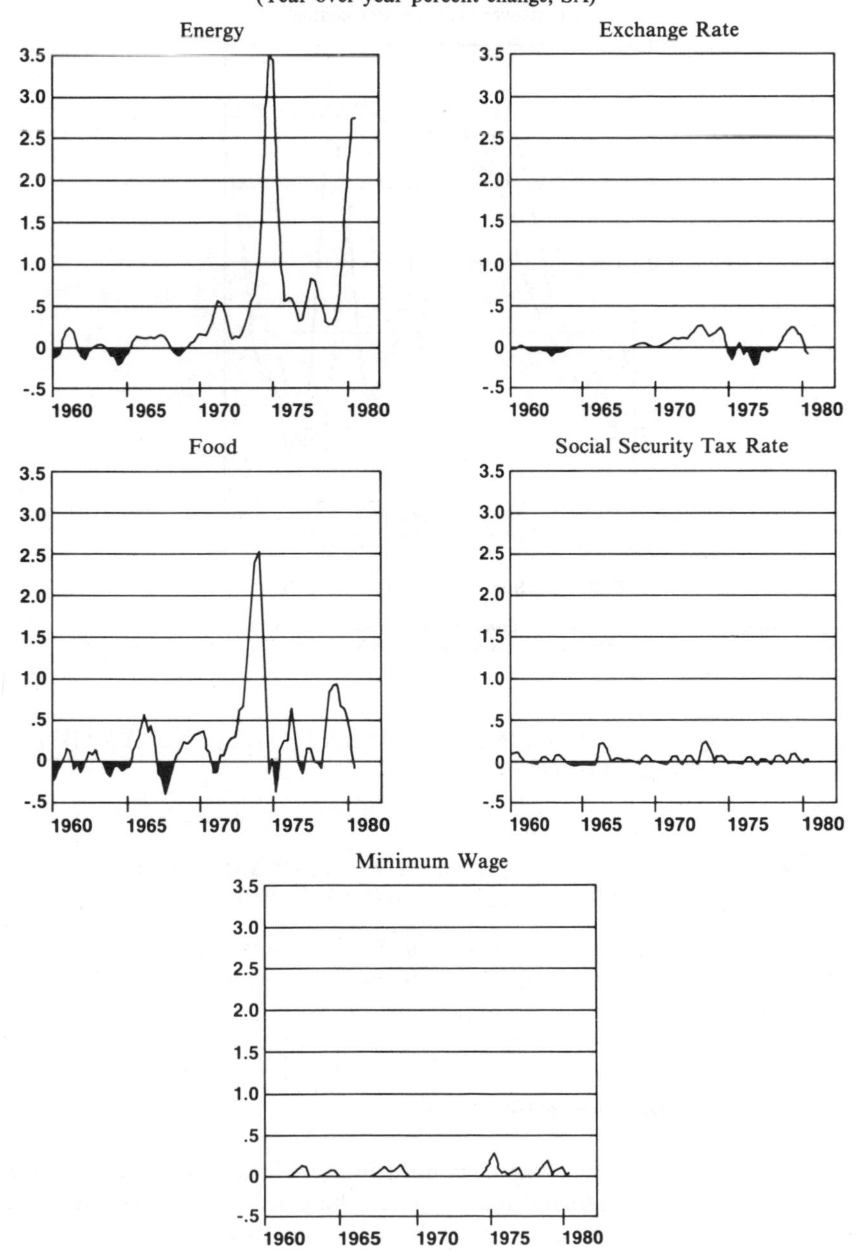

Chart 3.8
Demand Impulse* and
Demand Inflation Rate**
(Year-over-year percent change)

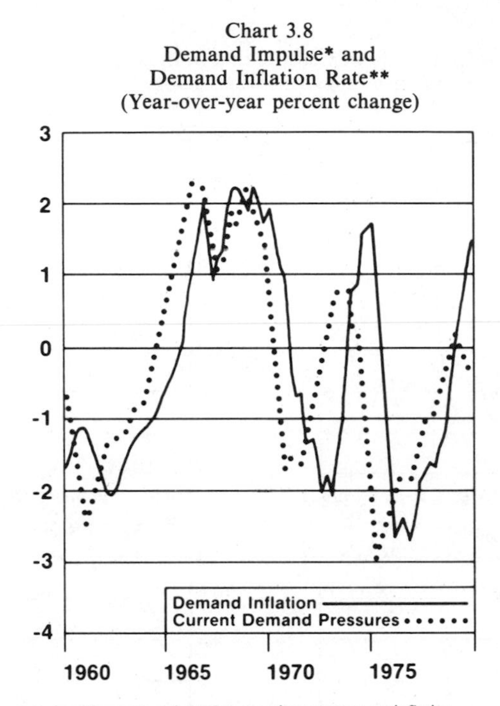

*Weighted average of current unemployment and current capacity pressures on inflation.
**The Demand Impulse is translated into the demand inflation rate with an average lag of four quarters.

$$(25)\ \dot{p}s_{RTWGF} = 15.4*\Delta RTWGF + 16.8*\Delta RTWGF_{-1} + 9.5*\Delta RTWGF_{-2} + 0.9*\Delta RTWGF_{-3}$$

and

$$(26)\ \dot{p}s_{MINWAGE} = .0004*\Delta MINWAGE + .001*\Delta MINWAGE_{-1} + .002*\Delta MINWAGE_{-2} + .003*\Delta MINWAGE_{-3},$$

where *RTWGF* is the tax rate for federal Social Security contributions, and *MINWAGE* is the federal minimum wage. The composite shock rate of inflation is calculated by combining (22) to (26).

3. The Demand Inflation Rate

The demand factor in the short-term inflation rate is measured by a function which relates current demand indicators to the price level. Since the actual inflation rate is largely determined by the core rate and shocks, direct correlations between demand measures and inflation would misspecify the effects. It is necessary first to identify the inflation that remains after allowance has been made for the core and shock elements. The procedure identifies the residual inflation rate by subtracting the core and shock rates from the actual values, and uses equation (27) to explain this residual through two of the more powerful of the demand variables in the model.

$$(27)\ \dot{p}_d = -7.7 + \Sigma_{t-7}^{t-1}(\alpha_t/(RU-RUADJ)) + \Sigma_{t-7}^{t-1}(\beta_t/(1.1-UCAPFRBM)) + 0.20*DMYPRICE - 0.05*DMYPRICECUM$$

$$\Sigma\alpha_t = 13.8,\ \Sigma\beta_t = 1.1,$$
$$R\text{-bar squared} = .91;\ DW = .75$$

where *RU* is the unemployment rate, *RUADJ* is an adjustment for demographic changes, *UCAPFRBM* is capacity utilization in manufacturing, and *DMYPRICE* and *DMYPRICECUM* are dummy variables to capture the effects of the price controls of the early 1970s. The mean lags are four quarters for unemployment and capacity utilization. The results are shown in Chart 3.8.

Chart 3.9a
Inflation "Residual" versus
Estimate of Demand Inflation Rate
(Percent)

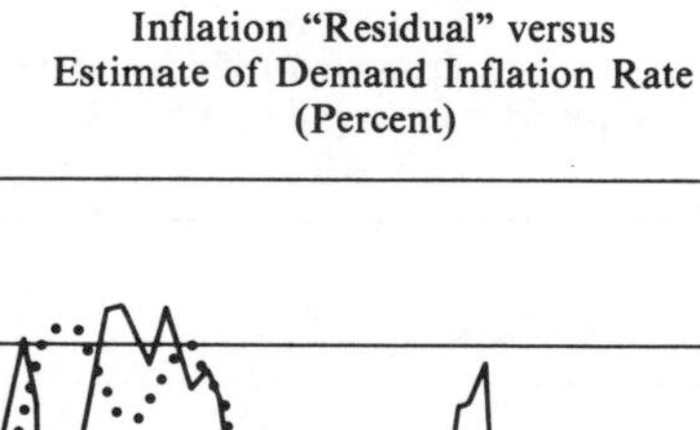
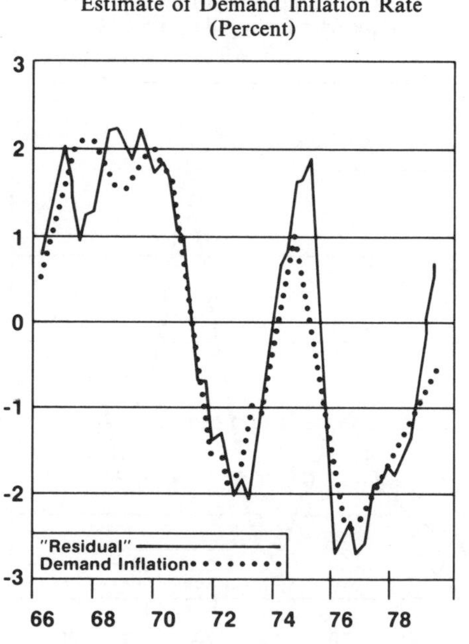

4. An Empirical Test

To be of analytical usefulness, the conceptual structure of core, demand, and shock inflation should account for a large share of the variation of the actual inflation rate. Equations for core and shock inflation are calculated from model simulations and thus are not the result of a statistical test. The demand equation is a statistical result, however. Since the equation is fitted to the residuals of price changes after estimated core and shock effects are subtracted, the test is quite powerful: if remaining error were large, a good demand equation could not be fitted. However, as Chart 3.9a shows, the residual inflation variable is mainly a demand variable and the equation explains 91% of its variance. Normalizing the equation by explaining actual price changes by the sum of the three inflation factors yields an R-bar squared of 97% (Chart 3.9b).

5. The Inflation Impulse Curve

Because the equations for the effects of shocks and demand have lags between their initial occurrence and their direct effects on the price index, the measures

Chart 3.9b
Actual versus Estimated Inflation Rate,
Consumer Price Index, 1966-79
(Percent)

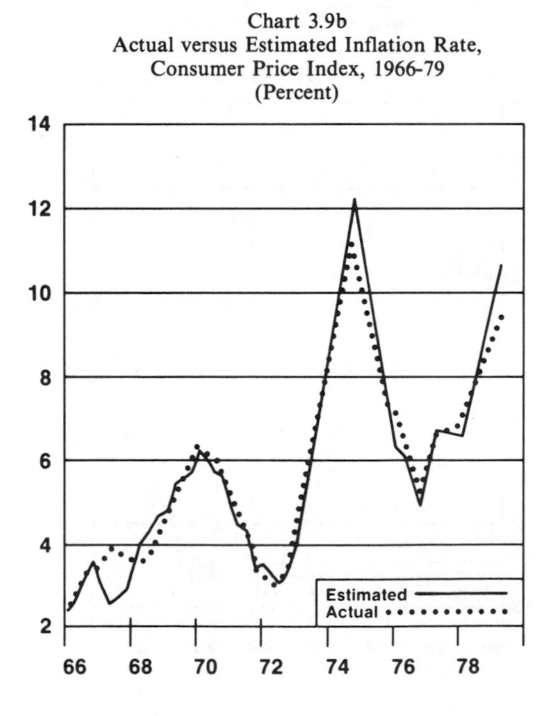

of p_s and p_d do not reflect what is happening in the current quarter but rather show the shock and demand patterns of the recent past.

Is it possible to define what is happening in the current quarter: what are the shocks and the state of demand that give rise to the later repercussions on the price level, and still later, on core inflation? The "Inflation Impulse Curve" measures the sum of the magnitudes of the several kinds of shock and of the demand factors as they enter equations (22-27), but without the lag structures. Each shock and demand variable is weighted by its full effect on the price level according to the equations after all lags, but it is the current quarter value which receives the full weight. The Inflation Impulse Curve portrays the timing of the origins of inflation troubles but does not show when the results occur. Chart 3.10 shows its historical record. Similar variables could be shown for individual shock and demand sources.

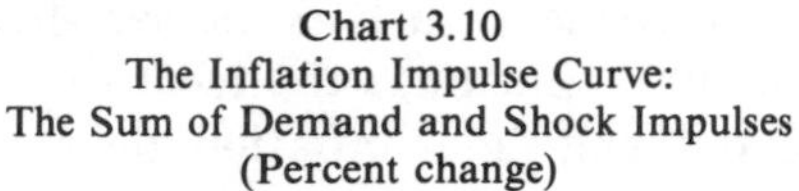

Chart 3.10
The Inflation Impulse Curve:
The Sum of Demand and Shock Impulses
(Percent change)

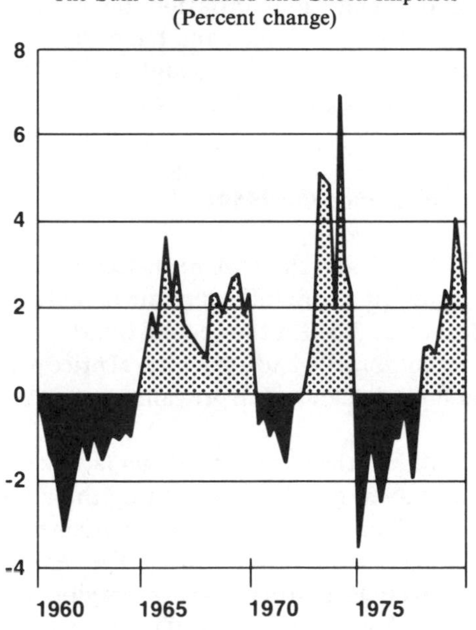

CHAPTER 4

HISTORICAL REVIEW OF CORE INFLATION

A historical analysis of the core inflation rate can help to explain the mechanisms and the reasons for the deteriorating performance of the last 15 years. The actual inflation record has been very volatile. There have been periods of dramatic improvement, such as the near-halving of the inflation rate between 1974 and 1976. But once the record is analyzed through the concepts of core, demand, and shock inflation, the periods of improvement prove to be almost entirely due to chance and temporary factors. Conversely, the periods of the worst inflation in 1974-75 and in 1979-80 are also seen to be temporary deviations above fundamental forces.

1. Core Inflation at the End of the 1950s

The Korean War of 1950-53 and the cost push-sectoral demand inflation of the mid-1950s left a legacy of a core inflation rate of 3.6% in 1957. The actual inflation rate also peaked at 3.6% in the second quarter of that year, but this figure contained some temporarily bad agricultural price performance and the lagged effects of the high demand that prevailed from late 1955 until early 1957.

For the years 1957 to 1960, the rise in trend unit labor costs averaged 3.1%. Equilibrium wage gains averaged 4.6%, fueled by the inflation experienced earlier in the decade. The extraordinary wage settlements of 1955-56 kept actual wage costs rising by 4% even during the severe 1958 recession. Productivity gave an average performance, averaging 1.5% trend growth, though decelerating over those four years and pushing unit labor cost gains to 3.8% in 1960.

Capital costs also rose considerably, particularly early in the period. Long-term interest rates rose mainly under the influence of tough policies even though inflation was moderate, producing relatively high real interest rates. Tax policy contained no significant moves during this period. The stock

Table 4.1
Core, Shock, and Demand Inflation: 1957-60
(Percent change)

	1957	1958	1959	1960
Unit Labor Cost Trend *(weight .65)*	2.8	3.1	2.8	3.8
"Equilibrium" Wage Gains	4.6	4.8	4.6	4.6
Actual Wage Gains	5.0	4.0	3.7	3.3
Price Expectations	2.0	2.2	2.2	2.1
Unemployment Rate (level)	4.3	6.8	5.4	5.5
Productivity Trend	1.8	1.7	1.7	0.8
Actual Productivity Gains	1.9	1.8	3.3	1.0
+ ***Capital Cost Trend*** *(weight .35)*	5.0	3.8	2.1	1.8
Actual Rental Price of Capital	4.4	-6.7	3.4	1.0
Aftertax Cost of Capital	-0.5	-13.4	4.8	1.6
Prime Rate (level)	4.20	3.83	4.48	4.82
New High-Grade Corporate Bond Rate (level)	4.45	4.02	4.77	4.68
Price Expectations	1.9	2.3	2.2	2.1
Dividend-Price Ratio—S&P 500 (level)	4.0	3.8	3.1	3.5
= ***Core Inflation Rate***	3.6	3.3	2.6	3.1
Shock Inflation Rate	0.6	0.1	-0.3	0.1
WPI—Farm Products	2.7	4.4	-6.1	-0.3
WPI—Fuels	5.4	-3.9	-0.1	1.0
Trade-Weighted Exchange Rate			0.2	0.4
Social Security Tax Rate (difference)	0.005	0.000	0.006	0.007
Minimum Wage ($/hour)	1.000	1.000	1.000	1.000
Demand Inflation Rate	-0.6	-0.5	-1.2	-1.6
Capacity Utilization in Manufacturing (level)	0.836	0.750	0.816	0.801
Unemployment Rate (level)	4.3	6.8	5.4	5.5
Consumer Price Index	3.4	2.7	0.9	1.5

market rose, cutting dividend yields, and thereby lowering the cost of equity capital. The capital cost trend slowed from a 5.0% rate in 1957 to a 1.8% rate in 1960.

The shock factor in inflation was mildly helpful in this period. Food prices fell after their unfortunate surge during the trough of the 1958 recession, a surge which produced the first cries of "stagflation." During the recovery of 1959-60, farm prices dropped by over 10%. Energy prices drifted lower. The dollar was still strong, even though the first serious payments deficits were emerging. Social Security taxes provided periodic shocks. But the total of shock inflation was near zero.

It was the demand factor that pushed the actual inflation results below the core rate. The recession of 1958 was quite severe, with unemployment peaking at 7.4% and the utilization rate of manufacturing averaging only 75% for the year. The recovery of 1959-60 was modest, avoiding unemployment below the natural rate and avoiding high industrial utilization. These weak demand conditions lowered the inflation rate by over a full percentage point per year between 1957 and 1960.

2. *Ending Core Inflation: Balanced Growth of the Early 1960s*

By 1961, the core inflation rate was down to 2.1% and edging lower. It eventually dipped below 1% in 1965.

How was this achieved? Given the current high core rate and the keen desire to reduce it, the accomplishment of the early 1960s is worthy of careful study. These years, which at the time were not considered years of outstanding economic performance, can now be seen more clearly as a kind of golden age for economic policy.

The almost complete elimination of core inflation had several ingredients. First, productivity performance was outstanding between 1960 and 1965. Labor productivity rose at an average rate of 3.5%, the best result of the entire postwar period. Once out of the recession of 1960-61, this was an era of strong investment growth and steady increases in the capital-labor ratio. The healthy economic recovery also prevented any cyclical dampening of output per hour. The average annual rate of wage increase, perhaps aided by President Kennedy's guidepost principles, fell to just above 3%. It was helped by an unemployment rate which was above normal until the final year of the period, and further affected by the previous record of price stability which kept inflation expectations low. The price expectations variable in the wage equation showed an average value of 1.7% for these years.

The trend in capital costs showed an equally positive and striking pattern. The improved inflation record and relatively accommodating monetary policies kept long-term interest rates stable and even left short-term rates at rather low levels in a rising economy. The stock market experienced a boom in the opening years of the decade which helped lower the cost of equity capital, but the crash of 1962 temporarily lost this particular benefit before the market resumed its rise.

In addition to low external costs for capital, the government undertook several major new policies which helped to lower the cost of internally financed capital. The introduction of the investment tax credit and liberalized depreciation methods in 1962 reduced the rental price of capital by 3.3%. By 1964, these tax incentive measures also began to show effects in terms of increased investment outlays which further helped productivity performance.

Table 4.2
Core, Shock, and Demand Inflation: 1960-65
(Percent change)

	1960	1961	1962	1963	1964	1965
Unit Labor Cost Trend *(weight .65)*	3.8	3.0	2.1	1.8	1.4	0.9
"Equilibrium" Wage Gains	4.6	4.4	4.2	4.1	4.0	3.9
Actual Wage Gains	3.3	3.2	3.2	2.9	2.6	3.4
Price Expectations	2.1	2.0	1.7	1.6	1.6	1.5
Unemployment Rate (level)	5.5	6.7	5.6	5.6	5.2	4.5
Productivity Trend	0.8	1.4	2.0	2.3	2.6	2.9
Actual Productivity Gains	1.0	2.8	4.3	3.4	3.5	3.4
+ ***Capital Cost Trend*** *(weight .35)*	1.8	0.5	-0.1	0.0	0.1	0.0
Actual Rental Price of Capital	1.0	-5.0	1.3	1.0	-1.5	2.2
Aftertax Cost of Capital	1.6	-8.6	11.3	2.9	3.1	5.3
Prime Rate (level)	4.82	4.50	4.50	4.50	4.50	4.54
New High-Grade Corp. Bond Rate (level)	4.68	4.42	4.23	4.25	4.40	4.54
Price Expectations	2.1	1.8	1.5	1.5	1.5	1.5
Dividend-Price Ratio—S&P 500 (level)	3.5	3.0	3.4	3.2	3.0	3.0
= ***Core Inflation Rate***	3.1	2.1	1.3	1.1	1.0	0.6
Shock Inflation Rate	0.1	0.0	0.1	-0.1	-0.2	0.3
WPI—Farm Products	-0.3	-1.0	1.8	-2.1	-1.5	4.4
WPI—Fuels	1.0	1.1	-0.5	-0.4	-2.7	1.8
Trade-Weighted Exchange Rate	0.4	0.9	1.9	0.4	0.0	0.0
Social Security Tax Rate (difference)	0.007	0.001	0.003	0.005	-0.002	-0.002
Minimum Wage ($/hour)	1.000	1.049	1.150	1.183	1.250	1.250
Demand Inflation Rate	-1.6	-1.1	-0.3	0.2	0.5	0.7
Capacity Utilization in Manufacturing (level)	0.801	0.773	0.814	0.835	0.857	0.895
Unemployment Rate (level)	5.5	6.7	5.6	5.6	5.2	4.5
Consumer Price Index	1.5	1.1	1.2	1.2	1.3	1.6

Capital costs contributed nothing to core inflation, being precisely stable. This left labor productivity gains free to offset the wage advances and gradually to remove the core inflation rate of 3% inherited at the beginning of the period. The unit labor cost trend fell to 0.9% by early 1965.

The demand factor was mixed during these years. The 1960-61 recession weakened markets, holding manufacturing utilization rates at an average of 79% and pushing the unemployment rate to 6.7% for the year 1961. In the years 1963-65, however, the demand factor began to add to inflation, as above-potential growth in real output began to tighten both capital and labor markets. Demand inflation averaged 0.3% per year over the entire period.

Shock inflation was absent in those happy years. The price of energy was stable, indeed edging lower. Food prices also showed little change, except for small drops in 1963 and 1964. The exchange rate rose, as the pound and various other currencies fell, to more than offset the appreciation of the German D-mark. The dollar was kept firmly pegged despite payments deficits. On the government side, payroll taxes were boosted substantially in 1962 and 1963, and the minimum wage also showed some upward revision. But putting together all the measured shock factors, the net contribution for the entire six-year span was almost precisely zero.

Could this "golden age" have been sustained through the rest of the 1960s? As the following section shows, historical forces began to take over and the happy period of balanced growth, with a slow closing of the gap of unutilized resources, was bound to come to an end.

3. *Core Inflation Begins Again, 1966-70*

If core inflation was almost eliminated in 1965, it had deteriorated to 4.1% by 1970. The process which destroyed price stability is clear enough: the military expenditures for the Vietnam War, which took on major dimensions in late 1965 and 1966, raised the level of demand to highly inflationary levels. The demand component of inflation had begun to reappear by late 1962, and was running at a 0.7% rate by 1965. Thereafter, it jumped to 1.4% and averaged 1.6% through the end of the decade. This demand component accounts for most of the deterioration of inflation in the early part of the period. Shock inflation remained small, averaging only 0.3% a year, mainly due to a large 1966 jump in payroll taxes, a 7.3% jump of food prices in 1966 (partly in response to military buying), and significant upward movements of the minimum wage in 1967 and 1968.

As the actual inflation rate began to be driven up by demand forces, price expectations started to deteriorate. Between 1965 and 1968, the deterioration was still small. Price expectations as shown in wage behavior rose from 1.5% to 2.4%; price expectations as they enter long-term interest rates advanced from 1.5% to 2.7%. Thereafter, expectations speeded up. By the end of 1970, price expectations of labor had jumped to 3.4%, of lenders to 3.9%.

Productivity began to show the first serious signs of retardation in 1967, growing at an average annual rate of only 1.2% for the years 1966-70. The escalation of expenditures on pollution abatement equipment seems to have had a particularly deleterious impact on productivity performance at that time. Productivity provided little offset for the accelerating wage gains, and helped push the unit labor cost trend from 0.9% in 1965 to 3.3% in 1970.

Table 4.3
Core, Shock, and Demand Inflation: 1965-70
(Percent change)

	1965	1966	1967	1968	1969	1970
***Unit Labor Cost Trend** (weight .65)*	0.9	1.0	1.3	1.7	2.6	3.3
"Equilibrium" Wage Gains	3.9	4.0	4.4	4.6	5.2	5.6
Actual Wage Gains	3.4	4.4	4.9	6.2	6.7	6.7
Price Expectations	1.5	1.7	2.0	2.4	2.9	3.4
Unemployment Rate (level)	4.5	3.8	3.8	3.6	3.5	5.0
Productivity Trend	2.9	3.1	3.0	2.9	2.5	2.2
Actual Productivity Gains	3.4	2.5	1.6	3.2	-0.2	0.1
+ ***Capital Cost Trend** (weight .35)*	0.0	0.9	2.1	2.2	3.7	5.6
Actual Rental Price of Capital	2.2	6.4	0.1	6.8	11.1	5.6
Aftertax Cost of Capital	5.3	3.8	-6.3	1.7	-1.3	-3.7
Prime Rate (level)	4.54	5.63	5.63	6.28	7.95	7.91
New High-Grade Corp. Bond Rate (level)	4.54	5.44	5.77	6.48	7.68	8.50
Price Expectations	1.5	1.8	2.2	2.7	3.3	3.9
Dividend-Price Ratio—S&P 500 (level)	3.0	3.3	3.2	3.1	3.2	3.8
= ***Core Inflation Rate***	0.6	0.9	1.6	1.9	3.0	4.1
Shock Inflation Rate	0.3	0.7	0.0	0.2	0.5	0.4
WPI—Farm Products	4.4	7.3	-5.6	2.5	6.4	1.7
WPI—Fuels	1.8	2.5	2.3	-1.1	2.0	5.3
Trade-Weighted Exchange Rate	0.0	0.0	-0.1	-1.3	-0.1	-2.5
Social Security Tax Rate (difference)	-0.002	0.014	0.003	0.001	0.004	0.000
Minimum Wage ($/hour)	1.250	1.250	1.387	1.583	1.600	1.600
Demand Inflation Rate	0.7	1.4	1.2	2.1	2.0	1.4
Capacity Utilization in Manufacturing (level)	0.895	0.911	0.869	0.870	0.862	0.794
Unemployment Rate (level)	4.5	3.8	3.8	3.6	3.5	5.0
Consumer Price Index	1.6	3.0	2.8	4.2	5.4	5.9

The rental price of capital also began to rise more rapidly under pressure from the response of long-term interest rates to inflation, war-induced strains on the financial system, dramatic stop-go monetary policies in 1966 and 1969-70, and the two-stage collapse of the stock market in association with those credit crunch episodes. As a result, the core inflation rate was up to 4.1% by 1970, while the actual inflation rate reached a substantially worse figure of 5.9%, principally due to the inflationary excess demand levels of 1968 and 1969.

4. Slow Deterioration, 1970-73

The core inflation rate edged up slightly from 4.1% in 1970 to 4.4% in 1973. This performance was obscured by President Nixon's price controls program of August 1971, which improved the actual inflation record from 1970's 5.9% bulge to a trough figure of 3.3% in 1972.

Worsening core inflation was in large part due to the persistent phenomena injected by price expectations into wages and capital costs. Even though unemployment rose to 6% as a result of the 1970 recession, wages kept rising at near 7% rates because inflation expectations had taken root in the period of excess demand. Wage controls seem to have made little difference.

The trend of capital costs also remained unfavorable. It had reached the 2-to-4% range in the years 1967 to 1969, surged in 1970 under the impact of the credit crunch and the collapse of the stock market, and then showed some small improvement to 4.4% in 1972-73. Only the tax cuts of 1971-72, including the restoration of the investment credit, helped to hold down the rental price of capital.

Actual productivity benefited from a cyclical upswing, averaging 3.4% annual gains in 1971-72. However, the productivity trend continued the downward path that had begun in the mid-1960s.

Excess demand became a problem once more in 1972 and 1973. Industrial utilization rates were driven up by domestic strength following the President's New Economic Policy and the worldwide boom of industrial countries. Unemployment reached full employment levels, but not an excess demand rate.

The actual inflation experience was considerably more variable than the behavior of the core rate. In 1971 and 1972, the price controls held down actual prices, while the shock inflation rate averaged a modest 0.7%. By 1973, the volatile elements took over, and the explosion of food prices following disappointing crops and the mammoth Russian wheat sales helped contribute to the creation of a 2.9% shock factor for that year. The other major shock of this period was the beginning of the end of the stable foreign exchange rate. In August 1971, the dollar lost its traditional parity, and the subsequent drop boosted the prices of imported materials and finished goods. The year 1973 also saw a large 1.4-percentage-point boost in Social Security tax rates, and the first alarming signs appeared in world oil markets to set the stage for the dramatic OPEC events at the end of that year.

The interval 1970-73, when the economic burden of the Vietnam War had passed its peak, created an opportunity for reversing the disturbing trend of the core inflation rate. The opportunity was missed. Capital costs created by the credit crunch of 1969-70 and the learning process determining wage claims boosted core inflation. The weakening productivity trend also was a factor.

Table 4.4
Core, Shock, and Demand Inflation: 1970-73
(Percent change)

	1970	1971	1972	1973
***Unit Labor Cost Trend** (weight .65)*	3.3	3.7	4.1	4.3
"Equilibrium" Wage Gains	5.6	5.8	5.9	5.8
Actual Wage Gains	6.7	7.1	6.5	6.2
Price Expectations	3.4	3.8	4.0	4.0
Unemployment Rate (level)	5.0	6.0	5.6	4.9
Productivity Trend	2.2	2.1	1.7	1.4
Actual Productivity Gains	0.1	3.1	3.6	1.7
+ ***Capital Cost Trend** (weight .35)*	5.6	5.5	4.3	4.4
Actual Rental Price of Capital	5.6	-0.1	2.6	11.8
Aftertax Cost of Capital	-3.7	-0.8	3.1	12.0
Prime Rate (level)	7.91	5.70	5.25	8.02
New High-Grade Corporate Bond Rate (level)	8.50	7.36	7.16	7.65
Price Expectations	3.9	4.2	4.1	4.1
Dividend-Price Ratio—S&P 500 (level)	3.8	3.1	2.8	3.0
= ***Core Inflation Rate***	4.1	4.3	4.2	4.4
Shock Inflation Rate	0.4	0.7	0.8	2.9
WPI—Farm Products	1.7	1.7	10.7	41.0
WPI—Fuels	5.3	8.5	3.0	13.2
Trade-Weighted Exchange Rate	-2.5	-2.9	-6.1	-5.9
Social Security Tax Rate (difference)	0.000	0.004	0.004	0.014
Minimum Wage ($/hour)	1.600	1.600	1.600	1.600
Demand Inflation Rate	1.4	-0.7	-1.7	-1.1
Capacity Utilization in Manufacturing (level)	0.794	0.784	0.835	0.876
Unemployment Rate (level)	5.0	6.0	5.6	4.9
Consumer Price Index	5.9	4.3	3.3	6.2

Demand inflation was hidden by price controls, but the suppressed inflation turned into catch-up inflation in 1974-75, after the controls collapsed as a byproduct of Watergate and the Presidential turnover. The food shock and the beginnings of the oil shock also helped set the stage for the dramatically worse experience in the following period.

5. Core Inflation Explodes, 1974-79

If the development of a core inflation rate of 4.4% in the years 1965 to 1973 was disturbing, the subsequent surge to over 8% by early 1979 was more worrisome. From 1973 on, the shock factors took over, initially worsening the actual inflation rate, but gradually also driving up the core inflation rate through their impact on expectations.

The rate of wage increase accelerated from 6.2% in 1973 to 7.2% by 1976. In the succeeding three years, it showed only a small further increase, as workers found themselves unable to maintain their real purchasing power in the face of the OPEC price increases. The moderation of wages was due to the high unemployment of the Great Recession of 1974-75 and the large labor force growth which kept unemployment high until 1978. Labor markets were fairly loose, and increasing economic uncertainties seem to have had a cautionary effect on union demands. President Carter's price and pay policy begun in October 1978 may also have had some moderating effect on the wages of unorganized workers.

While wages were moderate, the productivity offset was disastrous. Productivity growth could not hold up under the burden of energy costs and a stagnation in the growth in the capital stock. The gain in labor productivity from 1973 to 1979 was below 1% a year, so that the acceleration in the unit labor cost trend became extraordinary, moving from the 3.9% average of the previous interval to 6.6% for the later years.

The acceleration of capital costs was even more dramatic. The extended history of inflation was now beginning to work its way more extensively into long-term interest rates and price-earnings ratios. The capital cost trend, which had been rising by 4.4% in 1973, was rising at 10.3% in 1978 and 10.4% in 1979. Tax policy had done nothing to lower capital costs, indeed the temporary tightening of capital gains taxation probably served to raise equity capital costs even further. The changes in statutory corporate tax rates were small.

In the years 1976 to 1978, the actual inflation rate was below the core rate. The demand factor turned dramatically negative in the recession, lowering utilization rates to an average of 78% for 1975-77 and boosting unemployment to an average 7.7%. Shock inflation also backed away from the extreme values associated with the food and OPEC price explosions of 1973 and 1974. The improvement in food prices, which rose at only a 0.9% rate from 1974 to 1977, and a temporary recovery of the dollar associated with the dramatic improvement in our international trade position during the recession also helped to bring about the extraordinarily sharp improvement of inflation performance to a 6.1% average for the first two years of the recovery, 1976-77.

Better actual performance led policymakers to believe that the inflationary danger was reduced and that the double-digit experience of 1974 was a one-time phenomenon that could be identified with OPEC. But the experience of 1978-79, when the inflation rate surged ahead of the core rate again, was a sharp reminder that there really had been no improvement in the

Table 4.5
Core, Shock, and Demand Inflation: 1973-79
(Percent change)

	1973	1974	1975	1976	1977	1978	1979
***Unit Labor Cost Trend** (weight .65)*	4.3	5.7	7.4	6.6	6.4	6.5	7.0
"Equilibrium" Wage Gains	5.8	6.9	8.4	8.1	7.7	7.7	8.1
Actual Wage Gains	6.2	8.0	8.3	7.2	7.6	8.1	8.1
Price Expectations	4.0	5.0	6.5	6.8	6.6	6.4	6.7
Unemployment Rate (level)	4.9	5.6	8.5	7.7	7.0	6.0	5.8
Productivity Trend	1.4	1.1	0.9	1.4	1.2	1.2	1.0
Actual Productivity Gains	1.7	-3.2	1.9	3.5	1.6	0.5	-1.2
*+ **Capital Cost Trend** (weight .35)*	4.4	6.6	8.9	9.7	10.0	10.3	10.4
Actual Rental Price of Capital	11.8	16.8	8.9	10.3	10.9	10.4	10.5
Aftertax Cost of Capital	12.0	9.5	-4.1	7.2	6.3	5.4	7.2
Prime Rate (level)	8.02	10.80	7.86	6.84	6.82	9.06	12.67
New High-Grade Corp. Bond Rate (level)	7.65	8.96	9.01	8.33	8.06	8.88	9.86
Price Expectations	4.1	5.6	7.4	7.1	6.4	6.1	6.6
Dividend-Price Ratio—S&P 500 (level)	3.0	4.3	4.3	3.8	4.5	5.2	5.3
*= **Core Inflation Rate***	4.4	6.0	7.9	7.7	7.7	7.8	8.2
Shock Inflation Rate	2.9	3.8	1.2	0.6	0.8	1.0	2.3
WPI—Farm Products	41.0	6.5	-0.5	2.3	0.7	10.5	13.5
WPI—Fuels	13.2	55.0	17.7	8.3	13.8	6.7	26.6
Trade-Weighted Exchange Rate	-5.9	1.2	0.7	2.8	0.8	-6.0	-1.0
Social Security Tax Rate (difference) ..	0.014	0.004	-0.001	0.003	0.001	0.003	0.006
Minimum Wage ($/hour)	1.600	1.867	2.100	2.300	2.300	2.650	2.900
Demand Inflation Rate	-1.1	1.2	0.1	-2.6	-1.9	-1.2	0.7
Capacity Utilization in Manufacturing (level)	0.876	0.838	0.729	0.795	0.819	0.844	0.857
Unemployment Rate (level)	4.9	5.6	8.5	7.7	7.0	6.0	5.8
Consumer Price Index	6.2	11.0	9.2	5.7	6.5	7.7	11.2

fundamentals. The core rate was flat at 7.8% until it resumed its rise to reach a late-1979 peak level of 8.4%.

Capital costs were the most dramatic factor in the deterioration. As long-term interest rates kept rising, the stock market kept falling in relation to earnings, and tax moves were not particularly helpful. The rental price of capital accelerated from its 1974 trend of 6.6% to a sharply higher 1975 result of 8.9% and a 1979 figure of 10.4%. Labor costs, on the other hand, did not make a big contribution.

The year 1979 saw another round of worsening core inflation. OPEC increases together with the run-up of food prices made for a 1979 shock factor of 2.3%. Demand also reached inflationary levels late in 1978, with utilization rates approaching 87%. Inadequate capital formation had led to high utilization rates as excessively easy fiscal and monetary policies drove demand against the ceiling of productive potential. Thus, as the year 1979 closed, the core rate was at an all-time peak of 8.4%. Prospects were grim with more OPEC increases occurring and payroll tax increases ahead. Only the 1980 recession could prevent the core inflation from approaching double-digit levels.

CHAPTER 5

ENERGY AND CORE INFLATION

The energy revolution of 1973 was a principal cause of the worsening core inflation of the last decade. Oil prices may exercise a decisive influence on core inflation in the 1980s.

1. Energy Shocks and the Development of Core Inflation

The historical role of energy in the inflation process is shown in Chart 5.1. Until 1973, energy had little effect on the economy. Thereafter, the energy

Chart 5.1
Energy and Total Shocks: Effects on Prices
(Percent)

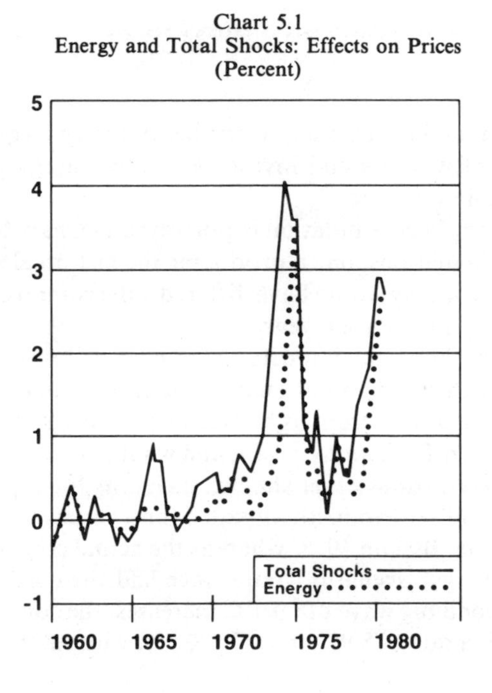

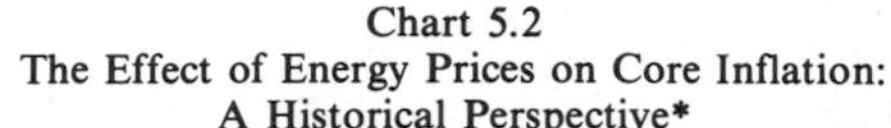
Chart 5.2
The Effect of Energy Prices on Core Inflation:
A Historical Perspective*

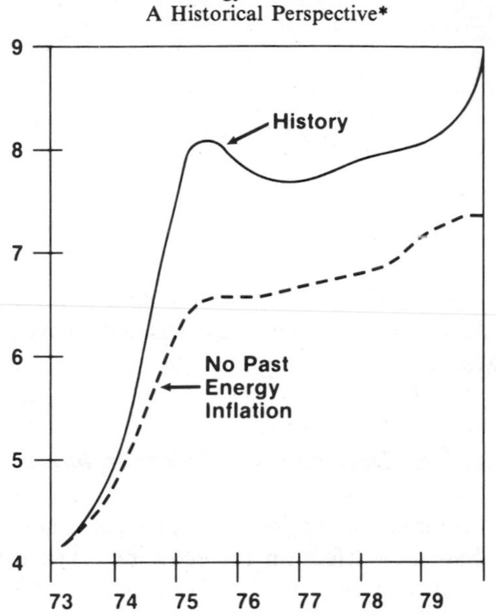

*Core inflation rate, history compared to results of hypothetical test in which energy prices rise no more rapidly than other prices.

component of the total shock component became very large. Gradually, via the expectations of workers and investors, higher energy prices converted themselves into core inflation.

The role of energy in core inflation is portrayed in Chart 5.2. It is based on two DRI model simulations, one reproducing the historical record, the other showing how the economy would have differed if the composite whole price of energy had risen by just 5½% a year.

The comparison shows the importance of energy, but also indicates that there is far more to the recent inflationary experience than this one factor. The core inflation rate had risen from its brief near-zero levels of the mid-sixties to 5% by the time the OPEC actions began, and would have continued to worsen anyway. There were various other shocks, including food, payroll taxes, and the decline of the dollar. Productivity faded for a variety of reasons of which energy was only one. By late 1978, whereas the actual core inflation rate was 8.0%, the "No Energy" scenario would have had the core rate at 6.8%. By 1980, after the second big wave of OPEC increases, the contrast is between an actual core inflation rate of 8.9% and a 7.1% rate without the energy troubles.

The need to adjust to higher energy prices also damaged the economy in other ways[1] (Tables 5.1-5.3). While the energy crisis was not the only factor pushing the economy off its equilibrium path in 1973-74, in its absence the economy would have suffered no worse than a year of stagnant GNP in 1974 and would have seen 1975 as the first year of recovery. By 1976, real GNP would have been 5.7% higher than in the historical tracking simulation. The 1980 recession would have been avoided, showing no more than some slow quarters.

The energy crisis was also largely responsible for the poor investment and productivity results of the years 1974 to 1980. In the "No Energy" case, the investment share averages a big 1.2% larger, and productivity would have advanced at a 0.9% better annual rate, a large share of the total productivity slowdown. The cumulative loss of potential GNP was 4.1% by 1980.

2. *Energy and the Future of Core Inflation*

The future price of world oil and its availability are the biggest uncertainties hanging over the U.S. economy. The enormous price increases in 1973 of OPEC-I and the equally massive increases in 1979-80 of OPEC-II have demonstrated that a multiplication of oil prices lies within the powers of the producers. There is no reason to believe that the dependence of the industrial world on OPEC oil supplies will diminish in the immediate years ahead, and so the risk of comparable instability of world oil prices is ever present. While, on the one hand, it may be against the self interest of the oil producers to wreak havoc with the industrial economies, their own political problems and the great diversity of viewpoints and political philosophies make a self-interest-based, quasi-rational outcome far from a certainty.

To illustrate the price effects of OPEC on the U.S. economy, three different model solutions have been run. The first assumes that OPEC prices will be stable in real terms from now on. Over the next few years, domestic energy prices will be rising because of gradual decontrol, but thereafter, energy prices would be rising no more rapidly than the price level as a whole. This is the most favorable of the scenarios tested.

[1]This analysis is a repetition of the work reported in greater detail in my recent book, *The Great Recession* (Amsterdam: North-Holland Publishing Co., 1978), Chapter 9, pp. 112-127, but performed on the current version of the DRI model. During the last three years, the model has become considerably more elaborate through the inclusion of the full energy sector as well as through various new supply formulations and a heightened sensitivity of the wage-price block. Despite various changes, the results are very similar to the figures reported in the earlier book.

The analysis by Mork and Hall produces similar magnitudes for the 1975 recession (Knut Anton Mork and Robert E. Hall, "Energy Prices, Inflation and Recession, 1974-75," *The Energy Journal,* July 1980, pp. 31-63).

Table 5.1
Summary of Tracking Simulation of the U.S. Economy
(Percent changes)

	1973	1974	1975	1976	1977	1978	1979	1980E
Prices								
Oil Import Price	23.6	205.0	11.6	-2.4	7.3	0.3	47.6	60.2
Wholesale Energy Price	13.2	55.1	17.7	8.3	13.8	6.7	26.6	41.9
Consumer Price Index	6.2	11.0	9.1	5.7	6.5	7.7	11.3	13.3
Core Inflation Rate	4.3	6.0	7.8	7.7	7.7	8.0	8.2	8.9
Shock Inflation Rate	2.9	3.8	1.2	0.6	0.8	1.0	2.2	2.4
Demand Inflation Rate	-1.1	1.2	0.2	-2.6	-2.0	-1.3	0.8	2.9
Supply								
Investment Rate (%)	10.4	10.7	9.8	9.7	10.0	10.4	10.8	10.5
Capital Stock	4.4	3.8	1.8	1.8	2.5	3.4	4.0	3.0
Output per Hour	1.8	-3.1	2.0	3.5	1.6	0.4	-1.2	-1.3
Potential GNP	3.0	3.3	3.3	2.6	2.6	2.9	3.3	3.2
Incomes, Output, Unemployment								
Real Wages	0.6	-2.6	0.3	2.1	1.7	1.3	-0.8	-1.4
Real Profits	17.5	0.2	-15.5	24.6	7.3	8.2	9.0	-15.3
Real GNP	5.5	-1.4	-1.3	5.9	5.3	4.4	2.3	-1.3
Unemployment (%)	4.8	5.6	8.5	7.7	7.0	6.0	5.8	7.5

E = DRI estimates of May 1980

Table 5.2
Summary of No Energy Trouble Scenario, 1973-80
(Percent changes)

	1973	1974	1975	1976	1977	1978	1979	1980
Prices								
Oil Import Price	10.0	5.5	5.5	5.5	5.5	5.5	5.5	5.5
Wholesale Energy Price	6.5	6.3	5.2	5.2	5.4	5.4	5.1	5.2
Consumer Price Index	6.0	8.1	6.4	4.9	6.0	7.5	10.0	8.9
Core Inflation Rate	4.3	5.4	6.2	6.4	6.7	6.8	7.1	7.1
Shock Inflation Rate	2.6	1.1	0.3	0.4	0.3	1.0	1.2	0.2
Demand Inflation Rate	-1.0	1.6	0.0	-1.9	-0.9	-0.3	1.7	2.5
Supply								
Investment Rate (%)	10.4	10.9	11.0	11.2	11.3	11.5	11.7	11.8
Capital Stock	4.4	4.4	3.9	3.9	3.8	4.1	4.2	3.9
Output per Hour	2.1	-0.1	3.2	2.3	1.3	0.5	-0.4	2.3
Potential GNP	3.0	3.4	3.8	3.6	3.6	3.7	3.6	3.3
Incomes, Output, Unemployment								
Real Wages	0.9	-0.1	1.7	2.3	1.7	1.2	0.1	1.1
Real Profits	17.2	7.5	-0.7	15.1	-5.2	2.7	3.8	-2.7
Real GNP	5.6	0.5	3.4	5.7	3.4	3.6	1.9	2.0
Unemployment (%)	4.8	5.2	6.7	5.6	5.8	5.6	5.8	7.0

Table 5.3
Economic Impact of Price Increases:
No Energy Trouble (1973-80) Compared to Tracking Simulation
(Percent changes)

	1973	1974	1975	1976	1977	1978	1979	1980
Prices								
Oil Import Price	-13.6	-199.5	-6.1	7.9	-1.8	5.2	-42.1	-54.7
Wholesale Energy Price	-6.7	-48.7	-12.5	-3.2	-8.4	-1.3	-21.4	-36.7
Consumer Price Index	-0.3	-2.9	-2.7	-0.9	-0.5	-0.3	-1.3	-4.4
Core Inflation Rate	0.0	-0.6	-1.7	-1.3	-1.0	-1.1	-1.1	-1.8
Shock Inflation Rate	-0.3	-2.7	-0.9	-0.3	-0.5	-0.1	-1.0	-2.2
Demand Inflation Rate	0.1	0.4	-0.2	0.7	1.0	1.0	0.9	-0.4
Supply								
Investment Rate (%)	0.0	0.3	1.2	1.5	1.4	1.1	1.0	1.2
Capital Stock	0.0	0.6	2.1	2.1	1.3	0.7	0.2	0.9
Output per Hour	0.3	3.0	1.3	-1.2	-0.3	0.1	0.9	3.6
Potential GNP	0.0	0.1	0.5	1.0	1.1	0.8	0.4	0.2
Incomes, Output, Unemployment								
Real Wages	0.3	2.6	1.4	0.2	0.0	-0.1	0.9	2.5
Real Profits	-0.3	7.3	14.8	-9.5	-12.5	-5.5	-5.1	12.6
Real GNP	0.1	1.9	4.7	-0.2	-1.9	-0.7	-0.4	3.3
Unemployment (%)	0.0	-0.3	-1.7	-2.1	-1.2	-0.4	0.0	-0.6

A second simulation corresponds to the baseline case. OPEC prices rise by 4% a year in real terms, keeping some continuing pressure on the core inflation rate. Demand management in the base case is more cautious than it was in the 1970s and is just about sufficient to offset the continuing pressure on the core inflation rate from the energy side.

The third scenario is a lot gloomier, with real energy prices rising at 10% a year. This is still a more favorable assumption than the actual experience since 1973: OPEC prices actually advanced at a 2.7% real rate between 1973 and mid-1980, though starting from a low base in relation to the U.S. price level. Under the 10% scenario, the refiners' acquisition price of foreign crude oil is $224 in 1990. It is hard to envisage a much higher price and still assume large imports.

Tables 5.4 and 5.5 summarize the results of these simulations. If OPEC prices rise no more than the U.S. price level, cautious demand management allows core inflation to improve at 0.23% a year for the next decade. This solution shows that energy is not the only factor in the continuation of core inflation. But improvement becomes readily feasible, and if other shocks are kept small, core inflation fades away to 6.6% over the decade. This OPEC assumption is very sanguine, however. The best assessments of the future world oil market do not suggest that a new equilibrium between oil and other prices has been reached or is near. In the first seven years since the OPEC

Table 5.4
Alternative Energy Scenarios, 1981-90
(Annual averages, percent)

World Oil Prices	Core Inflation	Consumer Price Index	Potential GNP	Productivity
0	7.8	7.0	2.4	1.4
4	8.5	8.2	2.3	1.2
10	9.8	9.8	2.1	1.0

Table 5.5
Alternative Energy Scenarios, 1990
(Annual averages, percent)

Real Energy Inflation	Core Inflation	GNP Deflator	Potential GNP	Productivity
0	6.6	6.7	2.3	1.4
4	8.0	8.3	2.2	1.2
10	10.8	11.9	1.7	0.8

revolution, oil reserves have not increased substantially: there have been few significant finds, and consensus judgments still hold out no better hope than constant domestic oil supplies.

An increase of real OPEC prices of 4% a year, an assumption that has considerable following in analytical circles, implies that core inflation will improve just slightly, to 8.0% by 1990. There would be a small loss in the growth of potential GNP and productivity as well, and the investment rate, the share of GNP that is invested in business fixed investment, would average somewhat below 10% compared to a share somewhat over 10% if there were no real OPEC increases.

If the OPEC increases average 10% a year, the economy is damaged severely, even if demand management avoids excess stimulus and other shocks remain on a minor scale. The core inflation rate would get worse, reaching 9.8% by the end of the decade. The growth of real GNP would be 0.3% less, and the productivity trend would be 0.4% smaller. Accumulated over 10 years, the loss of productivity is 4%, a loss on such a scale that it would reduce prospective real wage gains by one-half, from 1.4 to 0.7% for the decade.

The three simulations assume that demand management is similar and avoids overstimulus. Other shocks are assumed to be rather moderate, averaging less than 1%. Since domestic energy prices will be rising significantly as they move toward world market prices, there is little room for anything else to go wrong. Thus, the increases in agricultural prices and Social

Chart 5.3
Core Inflation Under
Three Energy Scenarios
(Alternative real world
oil price increases, percent)

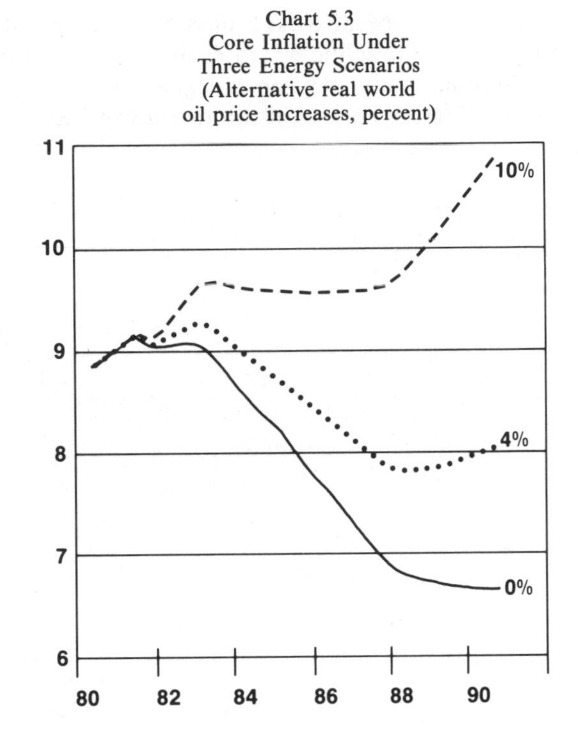

Security tax rates and any possible decline of the dollar all are assumed to be small. In other words, the non-OPEC assumptions are quite sanguine in the solutions, and if the worst of the OPEC scenarios were combined with other shocks or aggressive demand management policies, the deterioration in economic performance would be much more acute, of course.

3. Conclusion

Energy prices were at the heart of the deterioration of core inflation during the 1970s. Mismanagement of demand through budget and monetary policies as well as shocks such as food prices, payroll tax hikes and the decline of the foreign exchange value of the dollar also were factors, so it is simplistic to lay all the blame at OPEC's door.

Energy price will have a major effect on the trend of core inflation of the 1980s. If OPEC-II is followed by OPEC-III and OPEC-IV, there is no hope of improvement, indeed the deterioration would probably be quite dramatic.

Under more moderate energy scenarios, it is possible to largely neutralize the core price effects of energy through lower rates of operation of the economy and other policies. But under any scenario of significantly rising real energy prices, the task of bringing the core inflation rate down becomes very, very difficult indeed.

CHAPTER 6

IMPROVING CORE INFLATION: LIMITS OF DEMAND MANAGEMENT IN A WORLD OF SHOCKS

The last 14 years of worsening core inflation provide a discouraging background for discussion of the nation's inflation prospects. But there is the happy experience of the early 1960s, when the core inflation rate was completely removed over a period of five years. Have we lost the recipe for improvement? It would be premature to reach that conclusion when efforts to reverse the situation have just begun.

1. Baseline Prospects for the Economy

What are the prospects for the U.S. economy if policies are little changed? A DRI model solution has been developed which makes the following assumptions:

OPEC prices increase 4% a year in real terms, i.e. oil rises by the U.S. inflation rate plus 4%;

The statutory increases in Social Security taxes are allowed to occur, i.e, there is no rollback of the huge jumps in the income base and rate in 1981, and there are further modest increases throughout the course of the decade;

The federal budget grows by an average of 2.1% a year in real terms from 1979 to 1990, with transfer payments to persons growing somewhat more rapidly but grants-in-aid to states showing little increase. The defense budget in these assumptions rises by 2.6% a year;

Tax policy includes modest 1981 reductions of personal taxes and the beginnings of depreciation reform. Thereafter across-the-board personal income tax cuts slow the rate of increase in the real burden of income taxation from the 1.2% of the last decade to 0.6% for the first half of the 1980s;

Monetary policy expands nonborrowed bank reserves at 6.0% a year, which is sufficient to avoid credit disturbances while holding the growth of monetary aggregates to mildly disinflationary rates.

The 1980 recession in this base simulation is relatively mild, with unemployment rising only to 7.6% and dropping to 6.5% in the succeeding three years of recovery. The actual recession was somewhat worse, helping to hold down inflation. But OPEC was off to a much more damaging start for the decade, making the actual inflation prospects worse.

What would be the prospects for productivity, capital formation, core and actual inflation, financial markets, international trade position, and real activity under the baseline assumptions? Table 6.1 summarizes the results of a DRI model solution. Highlights for the years 1980 to 1990 include:

Potential GNP advances by 2.7%, a sharp contrast to the 3.5% average of the preceding 20 years;

The capital stock increases at a 3.2% rate, up from the 2.5% rate of the last five years but still well below the 4% long-term average;

Productivity growth remains sluggish, averaging a 1.8% rate of advance;

The core inflation rate shows no improvement, indeed worsens to over 9% for most of the next five years; the actual inflation rate (CPI) escapes from the current double-digit territory but still remains in the high 8.5-9% range through the mid-1980s. Some deceleration in both the core and actual inflation rates occurs over the rest of the decade;

The investment ratio, the percent of nominal GNP ploughed back into nonresidential fixed investment, averages 10.7%;

Real disposable income advances at a 2.8% rate, while real income per capita advances 1.9%;

Housing starts average 2.05 million units, which produces an increase in the nation's housing stock of just 1.6% a year;

The government deficit averages $14.9 billion a year, 1980-84, then turns to an average annual surplus of $35.6 billion, 1985-90;

Long-term interest rates, reflecting the high inflation, average 11.06% as measured by AA-utility bonds; and

Short-term interest rates remain very high as well, with the bank prime rate averaging 11.62%.

This baseline simulation may appear pessimistic in terms of some of the long-term trends embodied in it, but it is optimistic in its assumptions about various specific factors. OPEC prices and supplies, agricultural prices, unpredictable elements in consumer and business spending, stop-go policies by the Federal Reserve or the federal budget, regulatory policies, runs on the dollar, and other such factors could make the path more unstable and thereby also deteriorate the trends significantly. Major improvement in the structure of the labor market is also assumed by the end of the decade, partly based on the increased experience of the labor force. Thus, it is an optimistic trend projection.

Table 6.1
Baseline Prospects for the U.S. Economy: Some Optimistic Dimensions
Summary

	1980	1981	1982	1983	1984	1985	1986	1987	1988	1989	1990
Policy *(billions of current dollars)*											
Average Tax Lifetime (years)											
Producers' Durable Equipment	11.1	11.1	11.1	11.1	11.1	11.1	11.1	11.1	11.1	11.1	11.1
Investment Tax Credit (rate)	0.086	0.086	0.086	0.086	0.086	0.086	0.086	0.086	0.086	0.086	0.086
Corporate Profit Tax Accruals	75.1	83.5	97.5	105.2	112.1	139.9	163.7	189.2	195.1	197.4	224.3
Macroeconomic Effects *(percent change)*											
Real GNP	-0.7	2.3	4.3	3.1	2.6	3.2	3.9	4.7	2.7	2.2	3.0
Total Consumption	0.4	1.6	3.8	3.3	2.7	3.1	3.2	4.6	3.4	2.7	2.7
Nonresidential Fixed Investment	-1.9	-1.1	4.4	3.9	1.6	4.1	8.2	8.1	3.3	1.6	4.2
Investment in Residential Structures	-17.1	11.4	15.4	2.9	2.2	3.9	11.8	4.9	-6.1	-5.1	2.6
Government Purchases	1.2	1.3	2.2	2.0	2.2	2.4	2.5	2.5	2.5	2.6	2.4
Long-Run Supply *(percent change)*											
Labor Force	1.8	1.8	2.1	1.7	1.4	1.3	1.3	1.3	1.3	1.3	1.0
Capital Stock	3.0	2.5	2.7	2.8	2.7	2.8	3.4	4.0	3.8	3.5	3.5
Output per Hour	-2.0	0.4	1.6	1.6	1.9	2.5	3.3	3.9	2.3	1.8	2.6
Potential GNP	2.9	2.7	2.7	2.7	2.7	2.7	2.6	2.6	2.6	2.6	2.6
Inflation and Unemployment *(percent change)*											
Consumer Price Index	11.7	9.5	9.1	8.5	8.0	8.3	8.1	7.3	7.2	7.1	7.2
Average Hourly Earnings	8.7	9.4	9.5	9.7	9.7	9.6	9.2	9.0	9.0	8.7	8.5
Real Wages	-1.7	0.0	0.7	1.4	1.7	1.5	1.5	1.9	2.1	2.0	1.8
Unemployment Rate (rate)	6.8	7.5	7.0	6.7	6.7	6.5	6.3	5.6	5.3	5.4	5.4
Capacity Utilization (level)	0.808	0.811	0.851	0.858	0.850	0.862	0.879	0.882	0.869	0.855	0.865
Unit Labor Cost Trend *(weight .65)*	8.6	9.2	8.6	8.3	7.9	7.6	7.5	7.1	6.8	6.6	6.3
"Equilibrium" Wage Gains	9.1	9.8	9.9	9.9	9.7	9.5	9.4	9.1	8.8	8.6	8.4
Productivity Trend	0.5	0.6	1.2	1.5	1.7	1.8	1.8	1.9	1.9	1.9	1.9
+ ***Capital Cost Trend*** *(weight .35)*	10.2	9.9	10.8	12.0	11.9	10.9	10.1	9.5	9.0	8.2	7.2
Actual Rental Price of Capital	7.6	12.8	15.9	11.9	7.8	8.2	8.2	8.5	7.3	4.2	6.1
Aftertax Cost of Capital	-1.7	3.0	7.4	3.0	-0.9	-0.8	0.1	1.3	0.2	-3.3	-1.1
Prime Rate (level)	13.6	11.1	11.7	12.1	12.2	11.5	11.0	11.1	11.8	11.2	10.5
New High-Grade Corp. Bond Rate (level)	11.2	10.5	10.8	11.0	10.9	10.8	10.7	10.5	10.4	10.1	10.0
Dividend-Price Ratio—S&P 500 (level)	5.5	5.9	6.7	7.3	7.0	6.1	5.6	5.6	6.0	5.5	5.2
= ***Core Inflation Rate***	9.1	9.5	9.4	9.6	9.3	8.8	8.4	7.9	7.6	7.2	6.6
Shock Inflation Rate	2.6	1.9	1.4	1.1	1.0	1.3	0.9	0.9	0.9	0.8	0.8
WPI—Farm Products	1.9	8.2	7.8	7.2	6.8	7.2	7.0	6.5	6.2	6.0	6.1
WPI—Fuels	46.5	25.6	18.7	12.9	11.4	17.6	10.7	10.4	11.0	10.3	10.3
Trade-Weighted Exchange Rate	-1.4	-1.5	-1.5	-0.5	-0.3	0.2	0.2	0.0	0.0	0.0	0.0
Social Security Tax Rate (difference)	0.002	0.008	0.001	0.001	0.001	0.001	0.001	0.001	0.001	0.001	0.001
Minimum Wage ($/hour)	3.100	3.350	3.600	3.850	4.100	4.400	4.700	5.000	5.350	5.700	6.050

2. *Limits of Demand Management*

What would it take to reduce the core inflation rate through tougher demand management alone, given the apparently inescapable push from shock inflation? Table 6.2 summarizes a model solution in which the core inflation rate is brought down by 1 percentage point by 1985. To achieve this gain in the core inflation rate requires an increment of average unemployment of over 2% by 1985. Thus, demand management would have to aim at an unemployment rate of 8% following the small 1980-81 recession.

It is disappointing that the trade-off between unemployment and core inflation is only 2-to-1 even after five years, but it should not be all that surprising in light of the analysis. The economy's problems are not really solved except for the elimination of excessively aggressive fiscal and monetary policies. The imbalance between the supply of labor and capital continues so that the utilization rate of industry averages 82% in the years 1982-85, even though unemployment averages 7.9%. The unemployment level is clearly deflationary, but the utilization rate of physical capital is not far from its equilibrium rate. In other words, the imbalance in the structure of production, in which there is an inadequate supply of basic industrial capacity compared to the supply of labor, continues to be damaging and limits the benefits of holding down aggregate demand. Lack of improvement is also due to the

Table 6.2
The Effects of Demand Management on Core Inflation
(Difference from baseline path)

	1980	1981	1982	1983	1984	1985
		Difference in rate of change				
Core Inflation Rate	0.0	-0.1	-0.3	-0.6	-0.9	-1.0
		Percent difference in levels				
Real GNP	-1.0	-3.0	-4.0	-4.6	-5.1	-6.0
Total Consumption	-0.7	-2.5	-3.8	-4.7	-5.5	-6.5
Nonresidential Fixed Investment	-0.5	-2.4	-3.4	-2.4	-1.3	-1.0
Investment in Residential Structures	-0.2	0.6	6.2	15.0	21.3	20.3
Government Purchases	-2.1	-5.4	-8.7	-11.8	-14.4	-16.8
Imported Fuel Price	0.0	0.0	-0.3	-0.9	-1.6	-2.5
Personal Consumption Deflator	0.0	0.0	-0.3	-0.9	-1.6	-2.5
Output per Hour	-0.4	-1.2	-1.4	-1.2	-1.2	-1.5
Potential GNP	0.0	-0.1	-0.2	-0.4	-0.6	-0.7
Unemployment Rate*	0.2	0.9	1.4	1.6	1.8	2.1
Capacity Utilization*	-0.01	-0.04	-0.04	-0.03	-0.03	-0.04

*Difference in level

continuing shocks to the system from energy which indirectly serve to raise the noninflationary rate of unemployment.

The perpetual state of recession required by this approach also has direct costs in terms of productivity and potential growth. Low output discourages investment, so that the capital stock loses 0.4 percentage points of baseline growth. Productivity is off by 1.5% by 1980, and potential is down by 0.7%. Labor supply would be 0.1% smaller as workers become discouraged and cease to look for jobs.

Charts 6.1a and 6.1b show the results of other simulations to define the 1985 trade-off between demand management and inflation. The reader may be surprised to find a curve that still looks suspiciously like a Phillips curve. It should be noted, however, that with the traditional aggressive demand management policies which aim to hold unemployment below 6%, there is virtually no trade-off. In this region, the inflation rate deteriorates very dramatically so that the Phillips Curve ultimately does become vertical. However, at the more moderate demand management ranges, a trade-off remains even after five years: the increase in the price level is controlled by the

Chart 6.1a
The Effect of Demand Management on Core Inflation:
Core Inflation Rate Under
Different Economic Conditions
(Alternative average unemployment rates,
1980-85, percent)

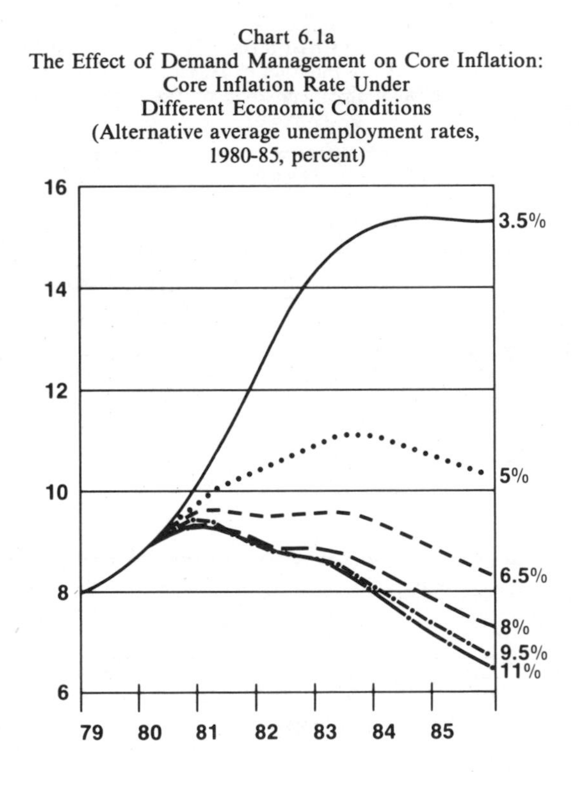

level of aggregate demand in relation to aggregate supply, and policy retains the ability to vary aggregate demand in accordance with the permitted increase in bank reserves and money supply and the degree of stimulus originating in the federal budget.

The curve shows that the achievement of a dramatically lower core inflation by 1985, to the 6% area, requires the maintenance of near depression conditions. Unemployment would have to be well over 10% from now until then, an economic condition which would seriously damage the economy in other ways, probably radicalize the electorate, and thereby imperil the capitalist system as we know it. Even to achieve more moderate anti-inflation goals through demand management alone poses only discouraging prospects. If the unemployment rate were maintained near 8% from now to 1985, inflation would be improved, but the core rate would still be near 7.5% at the end of the experiment.

Actual inflation rates would be slightly more sensitive to the higher unemployment than the core because of the more immediate offset provided by the demand component of inflation. However, actual inflation also

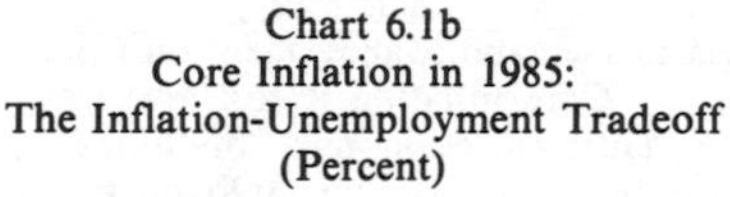
Chart 6.1b
Core Inflation in 1985:
The Inflation-Unemployment Tradeoff
(Percent)

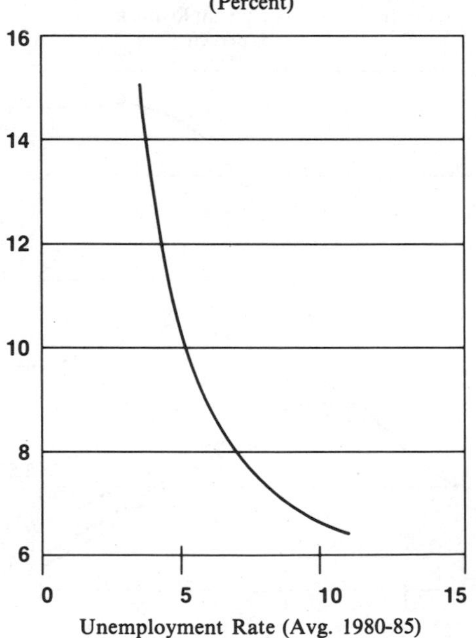

includes shock pressures, and although the weaker domestic economy might tone down the OPEC pricing strategy modestly, the energy problem could hardly be expected to disappear. Thus, with 8% unemployment, the consumer price index still increases at a 7% rate; even 10% unemployment does not produce less than a 6% rise in the CPI. It is very dubious that the political process would accept such a political strategy, regardless of who was president or which party controls the Congress.

3. Conclusion

In summary, the fiscal and monetary policies which the government employs to manage aggregate demand must create a constructive environment in which inflation can be improved, but they cannot, by themselves, solve the problem. Aggressive demand management, aiming at unemployment rates averaging 6% or less every year, make it impossible to have any other policy succeed. The inflation will simply become worse and worse, until the public despairs and forces politicians to adopt price controls. But even if demand management sets its gauges to achieve unemployment in the 6-to-7% area, the inflation problem is not solved. Indeed, given the probable shocks from energy, with a real OPEC increases of 4% a year, there would be no improvement in the core inflation rate. These exercises demonstrate that demand management must be careful and somewhat more conservative than it has been, but that it is beyond its capacities to accomplish an adequate improvement of inflation.

CHAPTER 7

REDUCING CORE INFLATION THROUGH HIGHER CAPITAL FORMATION AND BETTER PRODUCTIVITY

If demand management offers no satisfactory choices, can better results be achieved by actions on the supply side? Can capital accumulation be hastened and productivity performance improved? Can the rental price of capital be lowered? If sufficient benefits could be garnered from these sources, both the core rate of inflation and the actual rate would be improved. Combining such measures with fiscal and monetary policies that would hold aggregate demand to levels that would hold the core inflation rate stable, the result could be a reduction in the core inflation rate and a gradual reversal of the 15-year process which has brought us to the current impasse.

1. Corporate Tax Incentives

To explore these possibilities and to derive quantitative estimates, a series of DRI and core model simulations have been run. They show that it is possible to make significant progress by this method, but that it must be a long-term strategy followed for several years before results can be seen.

Three model solutions were developed: the first enlarges the investment tax credit, the second liberalizes depreciation methods for tax purposes, and the third combines these two measures. To identify the supply effects, the Keynesian multiplier associated with general stimulus is removed by tighter monetary policy and lessened government expenditures. Aggregate demand is allowed to expand along with the rise of potential, so that unemployment is little different in the comparisons. Thus the supply policies raise potential and actual output, creating the inflation improvement through lower costs. It is possible to make other choices: demand could be kept unchanged, so that the extra potential output creates a slacker economy and additional gains on inflation. Conversely, demand could be allowed to rise more than the gain in potential, so that the inflation improvement is lost as a result of the tighter demand situation. Since the Keynesian multiplier does apply to the investment stimulated by the tax incentives, unless offset by tightly disciplined demand policies, there is considerable danger of the latter outcome.

The total improvement in core inflation which can be achieved over 10 years, assuming the combined tax incentive policies and the tougher demand management policies, is 1.3%. While still far from a full solution to the inflation problem, it is major progress. To achieve even better results, it will be necessary to work on the shock inflation rate and its roots in the energy crisis, find additional policies to improve the supply of labor and capital, restore the growth in the stock of knowledge created by research and development, and improve labor productivity.

2. A More Generous Investment Tax Credit

In this simulation, the effective investment tax credit is raised by 2.7 percentage points in 1980 and thereafter. The direct revenue loss would be $4.5 billion in 1980, rising to $14.2 billion by 1990. This would boost nominal business spending on plant and equipment by almost $25 billion by the end of those 10 years. The rental price of capital would be lowered immediately which would begin to trigger extra business spending for equipment. The credit also would augment the cash flow of corporations and would thereby facilitate the financing of the extra outlays.

Table 7.1 summarizes the results of this simulation. It can be seen that the capital stock is boosted by an extra 2.7% by 1990, increasing the level of potential output by 1.0%, thereby also boosting the average growth of potential by 0.1 percentage point a year for the decade. The improved potential output creates a 0.1 point gain in the average rate of productivity growth and an average annual acceleration in real wages of 0.2 points.

The gain in real business fixed investment would average 2.6% a year for the years 1980 to 1985 and 4.6% a year for 1986 to 1990. There would be some spillover into higher consumption through the greater real purchasing power of consumers. Housing activity would be aided slightly because better price performance lowers interest rates, and housing is highly sensitive to this factor.

The reduction in the core inflation rate by 1990 is 0.7%. Much of this improvement comes very quickly when the investment tax credit is introduced because of its direct and major impact on the rental price of capital. This was the feature of the credit that had proved so helpful in 1962, when it played an important role in ridding the economy of core inflation.

Table 7.1
Reducing Core Inflation Through Investment Tax Credits
(Difference from baseline path)

	1980	1981	1982	1983	1984	1985	1986	1987	1988	1989	1990
Policy						Difference in Level					
Average Tax Lifetime (years) of Producers Durable Equipment	0.0	0.0	0.0	0.0	0.0	0.0	0.0	0.0	0.0	0.0	0.0
Investment Tax Credit (rate)	0.027	0.027	0.027	0.027	0.027	0.027	0.027	0.027	0.027	0.027	0.027
Corporate Profit Tax Accruals (% difference)	-6.6	-7.0	-8.1	-9.4	-10.8	-10.4	-11.9	-12.5	-12.9	-14.2	-15.6
Macroeconomic Effects						Percent Difference in Level					
Real GNP	0.1	0.0	0.0	0.2	0.2	0.5	0.5	0.5	0.8	1.1	1.2
Total Consumption	0.1	0.1	0.1	0.2	0.2	0.4	0.4	0.4	0.6	0.8	0.8
Nonresidential Fixed Investment	0.2	2.3	3.3	3.2	3.3	3.6	3.8	3.9	4.5	5.2	5.5
Investment in Residential Structures	0.4	1.8	1.2	0.3	0.9	2.1	2.5	3.5	5.3	6.6	5.4
Net Exports	0.6	0.8	2.6	4.5	5.6	7.4	10.9	16.3	21.0	21.8	22.5
Government Purchases	0.0	-1.8	-2.5	-1.9	-2.4	-2.1	-3.1	-3.9	-3.8	-3.7	-3.6
Long-Run Supply						Percent Difference in Level					
Labor Force	0.0	0.0	0.0	0.0	0.0	0.0	0.0	0.0	0.0	0.0	0.0
Capital Stock	0.0	0.3	0.6	0.9	1.2	1.4	1.6	1.9	2.1	2.4	2.7
Output per Hour	0.0	0.0	0.0	0.1	0.2	0.4	0.3	0.4	0.7	0.8	0.8
Potential GNP	0.0	0.0	0.1	0.2	0.3	0.5	0.6	0.7	0.8	0.9	1.0
Inflation and Unemployment						Difference in Rate of Change					
Core Inflation Rate	-0.1	-0.3	-0.3	-0.3	-0.4	-0.4	-0.5	-0.5	-0.6	-0.7	-0.7
						Percent Difference in Level					
Consumer Price Index	0.0	-0.1	-0.2	-0.3	-0.4	-0.6	-0.9	-1.2	-1.5	-1.9	-2.2
Average Hourly Earnings	0.0	0.0	-0.1	-0.1	-0.2	-0.3	-0.5	-0.7	-0.9	-1.2	-1.4
Real Wages	0.0	0.1	0.1	0.2	0.3	0.4	0.5	0.6	0.7	0.9	1.0
Unemployment Rate (difference in level)	0.0	0.0	0.0	0.0	0.0	0.0	0.0	0.1	0.0	-0.1	-0.1
Capacity Utilization (difference in level)	-0.002	-0.005	-0.009	-0.012	-0.015	-0.018	-0.023	-0.024	-0.022	-0.022	-0.028
Financial Markets						Difference in Level					
Rental Price of Capital (% difference)	-2.9	-2.9	-3.1	-3.7	-4.6	-5.3	-6.5	-7.8	-8.9	-9.7	-10.5
Prime Rate	-0.16	-0.11	0.19	0.19	0.04	0.01	-0.03	-0.16	-0.27	-0.23	-0.06
New High-Grade Corporate Bond Rate	0.00	-0.04	-0.06	-0.09	-0.14	-0.20	-0.25	-0.32	-0.37	-0.38	-0.37

3. More Liberal Depreciation

In the second simulation, the average tax lifetime of producers' durable equipment is reduced by four years, beginning in 1980. This directly lowers corporate profit tax accruals by $5.7 billion immediately and by $17.8 billion by the end of the decade. The liberalized tax laws also have a strong impact on capital costs. The rental price of capital is lowered by 4.4% in 1980 and continues to be lowered at a rate of an additional full percentage point a year between 1980 and 1990. As a result, nominal spending on plant and equipment is boosted by $7.1 billion in 1981 and $44.3 billion by 1990.

The long-run impact on supply is modestly greater than the investment tax credit case. The capital stock is raised by 4.3% by 1990, and potential output by 1.5%.

The lower rental price of capital and improved productivity path reduce the core rate of inflation by an average 0.6% over the decade. Again, given the direct initial benefit of the policy on the rental price of capital, much of the reduction is almost immediate. The productivity effect then helps to sustain the lower core rate over the next 10 years.

4. The Combined Policy

The third simulation imposes the more generous investment tax credit and the more liberal depreciation allowances in order to identify a full supply benefit on the core inflation rate. Table 7.3 summarizes this simulation. The increase in investment is very sizable, reaching almost a 14% increment for the years 1989 and 1990. This $73 billion gain in nominal investment outlays is achieved through a full-model reduction in corporate tax collections of similar amount, a very large corporate tax reduction equal to 33% of baseline revenues.

The large increase in investment over the decade boosts the capital stock by 7.2% by the end of the period. The extra capital produces an increase in potential GNP of 2.6%, and boosts the growth rates of both potential and productivity by 0.2 percentage points a year for the decade.

Real wages are higher by 2.3%, and better purchasing power produces a modest gain in consumption by the end of the decade. More favorable unit labor costs create a 10.5% improvement in real exports. Even state and local governments get a small benefit from the improved real purchasing power and the increase of their real tax base. The investment incentives initially lower interest rates because the cash flow benefits precede the spending increases. Later on, interest rates are lowered because prices have improved. Housing is helped at the beginning, hurt in 1982-83, but helped again thereafter.

Table 7.2
Reducing Core Inflation Through Liberalized Depreciation
(Difference from baseline path)

	1980	1981	1982	1983	1984	1985	1986	1987	1988	1989	1990
Policy	Difference in Level										
Average Tax Lifetime (years) of Producers Durable Equipment	-4.0	-4.0	-4.0	-4.0	-4.0	-4.0	-4.0	-4.0	-4.0	-4.0	-4.0
Investment Tax Credit (rate)	0.000	0.000	0.000	0.000	0.000	0.000	0.000	0.000	0.000	0.000	0.000
Corporate Profit Tax Accruals (% difference)	-8.5	-7.1	-8.8	-13.8	-14.6	-13.2	-16.0	-16.7	-16.7	-18.8	-19.6
Macroeconomic Effects	Percent Difference in Level										
Real GNP	0.1	0.3	0.4	0.3	0.3	0.4	0.3	0.4	1.1	1.3	1.7
Total Consumption	0.1	0.2	0.1	0.0	0.1	0.2	0.1	0.1	0.5	0.7	1.0
Nonresidential Fixed Investment	0.3	3.6	5.2	3.9	4.1	5.5	5.7	5.8	7.3	9.0	9.8
Investment in Residential Structures	0.7	3.9	1.0	-3.6	-0.5	2.9	1.4	1.9	6.2	10.1	12.5
Net Exports	0.6	-0.5	2.2	6.3	8.1	10.9	16.4	21.7	25.5	25.8	26.2
Government Purchases	0.0	-1.8	-1.6	-0.7	-2.1	-3.5	-4.2	-4.7	-4.6	-6.0	-6.2
Long-Run Supply	Percent Difference in Level										
Labor Force	0.0	0.0	0.0	0.0	0.0	0.0	0.0	0.0	0.0	0.0	0.0
Capital Stock	0.0	0.4	1.0	1.3	1.6	2.0	2.3	2.6	3.1	3.7	4.3
Output per Hour	0.0	0.2	0.2	0.1	0.3	0.6	0.4	0.6	1.0	1.3	1.4
Potential GNP	0.0	0.0	0.1	0.3	0.5	0.6	0.8	0.9	1.1	1.3	1.5
Inflation and Unemployment	Difference in Rate of Change										
Core Inflation Rate	-0.1	-0.4	-0.4	-0.4	-0.6	-0.7	-0.7	-0.8	-0.9	-1.0	-1.0
	Percent Difference in Level										
Consumer Price Index	-0.1	-0.1	-0.2	-0.3	-0.6	-0.8	-1.1	-1.5	-2.0	-2.4	-2.9
Average Hourly Earnings	0.0	0.0	0.0	0.0	-0.1	-0.3	-0.6	-0.9	-1.3	-1.7	-2.1
Real Wages	0.0	0.1	0.2	0.3	0.4	0.5	0.6	0.7	0.9	1.0	1.2
Unemployment Rate (difference in level)	0.0	-0.1	-0.1	0.0	0.1	0.1	0.1	0.2	0.1	0.0	0.0
Capacity Utilization (difference in level)	-0.005	-0.002	-0.007	-0.020	-0.020	-0.019	-0.031	-0.035	-0.028	-0.029	-0.036
Financial Markets	Difference in Level										
Rental Price of Capital (% difference)	-4.4	-4.6	-4.2	-6.3	-8.1	-8.4	-9.9	-12.0	-13.5	-14.5	-15.7
Prime Rate	-0.36	-0.24	0.81	0.73	-0.02	0.21	0.46	-0.12	-0.64	-0.67	-0.82
New High-Grade Corporate Bond Rate	-0.02	-0.03	-0.01	-0.02	-0.17	-0.31	-0.37	-0.47	-0.56	-0.58	-0.58

Table 7.3
Reducing Core Inflation Through Investment Tax Credits
and Liberalized Depreciation
(Difference from baseline path)

	1980	1981	1982	1983	1984	1985	1986	1987	1988	1989	1990
Policy	Difference in Level										
Average Tax Lifetime (years) of Producers Durable Equipment	-4.0	-4.0	-4.0	-4.0	-4.0	-4.0	-4.0	-4.0	-4.0	-4.0	-4.0
Investment Tax Credit (rate)	0.027	0.027	0.027	0.027	0.027	0.027	0.027	0.027	0.027	0.027	0.027
Corporate Profit Tax Accruals (% difference)	-15.7	-15.4	-17.9	-24.1	-24.7	-22.3	-25.4	-26.6	-27.8	-31.0	-32.7
Macroeconomic Effects	Percent Difference in Level										
Real GNP	0.1	0.3	0.3	0.2	0.7	1.2	1.4	1.8	2.7	3.3	3.7
Total Consumption	0.1	0.3	0.2	0.0	0.4	0.7	0.7	0.9	1.4	1.8	2.1
Nonresidential Fixed Investment	0.4	5.7	8.5	7.0	7.5	9.8	10.2	10.6	12.5	14.6	15.6
Investment in Residential Structures	1.2	5.6	1.5	-4.5	0.0	4.6	2.2	2.5	7.2	10.1	9.9
Net Exports	1.5	1.0	5.2	11.3	11.6	14.1	20.4	27.1	32.6	34.1	35.7
Government Purchases	-0.3	-3.7	-4.8	-2.9	-3.3	-4.3	-3.8	-3.4	-3.4	-3.3	-2.9
Long-Run Supply	Percent Difference in Level										
Labor Force	0.0	0.0	0.0	0.0	0.0	0.0	0.1	0.1	0.1	0.1	0.1
Capital Stock	0.0	0.7	1.6	2.2	2.7	3.4	4.1	4.7	5.5	6.4	7.2
Output per Hour	0.0	0.2	0.2	0.2	0.8	1.2	1.4	1.9	2.4	2.8	3.3
Potential GNP	0.0	0.0	0.2	0.5	0.8	1.1	1.4	1.6	1.9	2.2	2.6
Inflation and Unemployment	Difference in Rate of Change										
Core Inflation Rate	-0.2	-0.7	-0.7	-0.8	-1.0	-1.0	-1.0	-1.1	-1.3	-1.3	-1.3
	Percent Difference in Level										
Consumer Price Index	-0.1	-0.3	-0.4	-0.6	-1.0	-1.4	-1.9	-2.5	-3.0	-3.5	-4.0
Average Hourly Earnings	0.0	0.0	-0.1	-0.2	-0.4	-0.7	-1.0	-1.4	-1.7	-2.0	-2.2
Real Wages	0.1	0.2	0.3	0.4	0.6	0.9	1.1	1.3	1.6	2.0	2.3
Unemployment Rate (difference in level)	0.0	-0.1	-0.1	0.1	0.1	0.0	0.0	0.0	-0.2	-0.4	-0.4
Capacity Utilization (difference in level)	-0.010	-0.013	-0.017	-0.032	-0.030	-0.027	-0.038	-0.043	-0.039	-0.042	-0.053
Financial Markets	Difference in Level										
Rental Price of Capital (% difference)	-7.1	-7.5	-7.1	-9.8	-12.1	-12.5	-14.4	-17.0	-18.8	-20.0	-21.4
Prime Rate	-0.51	-0.30	1.09	0.96	-0.07	0.27	0.62	-0.11	-0.63	-0.56	-0.58
New High-Grade Corporate Bond Rate	-0.04	-0.10	-0.08	-0.14	-0.31	-0.43	-0.44	-0.49	-0.56	-0.53	-0.46

The core inflation rate shows a very significant improvement. For the final three years, 1988-90, the core inflation rate is reduced by 1.3 points. While this may seem a still modest gain, it does represent a sizable reduction. The improvement in the actual inflation rate is similar. The cumulative reduction in the level of the consumer price index is 4% by 1990, or an average improvement of 0.4 points in the annual rate of increase. The better productivity performance affects unit labor costs directly and thereby lowers the costs of many products.

Even the shock inflation rate receives some benefit from the improved overall performance. The model exercise was carried out with the simulation rules of the DRI macro model which can be applied to agricultural and world energy prices. Since the world oil price was defined to increase at 4% a year in real terms, there is a feedback from better U.S. domestic inflation performance to world oil prices. Similarly, while agricultural prices may be affected by the weather and other uncontrollables, there is a strong long-term

Chart 7.1
The Impact of Tax Incentives
on Core Inflation
(Year-over-year percent change, SA)

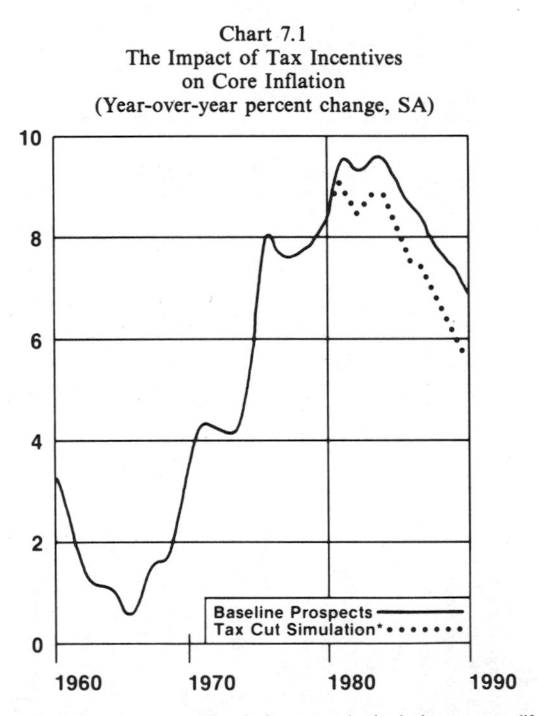

*Assumes a 2.7 point increase in the investment tax credit and a four-year reduction in the average tax lifetime of producers' plant and equipment relative to base, 1980-90.

association between the movement of the price level as a whole and the prices collected by farmers. Other elements of shock inflation, including the dollar exchange rate and minimum wages, also show a small benefit. As a result, the total shock factor in inflation is lowered by an average of about 0.1 point a year in this exercise.

Cautious demand management which holds unemployment at about 6.5% for most of the decade plus strong measures to stimulate business capital formation can lower the baseline core inflation rate by a full percentage point, while simultaneously creating a real wage gain of 2.3% and higher real output. Clearly other combinations of benefits from the policies could be achieved. Greater progress against core inflation could be accomplished by sacrificing the real output and income gains, using the slack instead to maintain looser product and labor markets. For example, if money and fiscal policies get tightened to hold real wages nearly unchanged, the improvement in core inflation could be boosted another full percentage point, from 1.3 to 2.3 percentage points. But even under that approach, core inflation remains far higher for most of the 1980s than it was just a few years ago. Nor is there any restoration of the conditions of the "golden" age of the first half of the 1960s, when core inflation was almost totally removed from the system.

The remaining core inflation rate shows that demand management and better capital formation are not sufficient to deal with the entire problem. To make further progress, at least three other approaches must be devised. First, the energy factor must be neutralized through conservation, better technology, or new discoveries. If the push from shock inflation could be eliminated, the improvement that becomes possible for the core rate becomes substantially greater. Besides energy, domestic government policies would also have to become far more constructive than they have been in recent years in such fields as payroll taxation, farm policies, and regulation.

Second, the nation also will have to improve its investment in science and technology. During the years 1957 to 1967, the stock of R&D grew at a 5.8% rate. Since 1967, its growth has slowed to 2.8%, and in the last two years it has averaged near zero. The loss in potential GNP growth associated with this lagging effort in science and technology affects the productivity of labor and capital and thereby worsens the core inflation. A return to more normal investment levels in R&D would make a measurable contribution to the reduction of the core inflation rate.

Finally, the total level of personal taxation needs to be re-examined. While the DRI model equations do not suggest high elasticities for the supply of labor with regard to the tax burden, there is a measurable loss of work associated with rising taxes. Further, the model equations include a loss of productivity associated with rising personal and payroll taxes.

This chapter has provided a quantitative exploration of one particular set of tax policies and their potential benefit in reducing the core inflation rate. We saw in the early 1960s that investment incentives work: the level of business investment in plant and equipment increased substantially after the 1962 measures, and productivity performed extraordinarily well. With demand management also on the cautious side, it was possible to get rid of the core inflation rate. Given the total circumstances confronting our economy today, the policies analyzed here certainly deserve the most earnest consideration.

CHAPTER 8

POLICIES TO BRING CORE INFLATION DOWN TO 5%

The preceding chapter explored the effects of limited tax measures designed to stimulate corporate capital formation. Reductions in the economic lives used for depreciation and modest increases in investment tax credits were applied in an economy benefiting from cautious demand management. The tax measures represented a $10.3 billion reduction in the 1980 economy. The results were encouraging but moderate: even with unemployment held in the 6½-to-7% range, the improvement in the core inflation rate was only 1% by the mid-1980s. Those exercises followed the methodology of using demand management to hold the unemployment rate unchanged in order to isolate the pure supply-economics effects. It also assumed that the real increase of energy prices was beyond policy influence, which put quite discouraging limits on any improvement in the core inflation rate.

Following completion of those studies, Senator Bentsen, Chairman of the Joint Economic Committee, requested a fuller exploration of possibilities which would set aside the political and budget constraints which limit tax actions to modest scale. He posed the question: what would it take to bring the core inflation rate down dramatically, not allowing political constraints to rule out possible solutions?

Making the variations in policy much larger, a series of simulations of the 800-equation DRI Quarterly Econometric Model of the U.S. Economy and its Core Inflation Model explored a broader range of policy options. The problem was posed as follows: what will it take to lower the core inflation rate to less than 5% by 1990? With that objective as given, the goal becomes how to minimize the unemployment required to achieve it, using various policy alternatives both on the supply and demand management sides.

Three cases were analyzed through a series of policy simulations to find the best solutions that would meet the pre-determined anti-inflation goal. In Case 1, policy is confined to the traditional demand management. Government spending is reduced to hold down aggregate demand to such a degree that the core inflation objective is reached. In Case 2, a very large tax reduction to stimulate corporate capital formation is applied at the beginning of the period, large enough to bring down the core inflation to the specified goal of less than 5% by the end of the decade. In Case 3, it is assumed that enough progress is made on the oil problem to hold OPEC prices to a constant real level defined in terms of U.S. inflation. The same supply-side tax cut is then applied, but because the shock element of inflation from OPEC is reduced, unemployment does not have to be kept quite so high, though still above the rates considered desirable in the past.

The conclusions of this set of exercises are clear:

(1) Demand management alone—budget and money supply control—imposes enormous social burdens to achieve the desired goal of bringing core inflation down to 5% by 1990.

(2) Supply measures to boost industrial capital formation make it possible to reach the core inflation goal with considerably less unemployment, but the measures are very large and unemployment must be kept above historical rates.

(3) A solution to the energy problem would open up a far more attractive set of choices, and would allow policy to operate the economy if not at full employment, at least with unemployment that is in the range of historical experience. The task left to new manpower policies would be of a magnitude that should be doable.

1. Case 1: Demand Management Only

Through a series of model simulation exercises, the level of government spending for goods and services was estimated low enough to achieve the core inflation target of less than 5% by 1990. With sufficiently restrictive policies, the economy would operate with considerable slack throughout the decade. High unemployment and low utilization rates of industrial capacity would serve to gradually disinflate the economy. Sensitive prices would remain relatively low. The wage increases of unorganized workers would slow down because of continuing excess unemployment. The more sluggish, cost-based prices would gradually respond to lower labor costs. Ultimately, even the contracts of the most strongly organized workers would show diminishing gains because of the improved price performance (Table 8.1).

The necessary budget policy is very restrictive indeed, with federal government spending as a whole in 1990 down to 19.7% of GNP. This is much lower than 1980's estimated 23.0% federal share. It implies an increase in total spending of just 0.5% a year in real terms. Its attainment is inconsistent with

Table 8.1
Simulation Results: Demand Management Only
(Average annual rates of change)

	1980	1981	1982	1983	1984	1985	1986	1987	1988	1989	1990
Policy											
Average Tax Lifetime, Equipment (years)	11.1	11.1	11.1	11.1	11.1	11.1	11.1	11.1	11.1	11.1	11.1
Average Tax Lifetime, Buildings (years)	22.8	22.8	22.8	22.8	22.8	22.8	22.8	22.8	22.8	22.8	22.8
Investment Tax Credit Rate (percent)	8.6	8.6	8.6	8.6	8.6	8.6	8.6	8.6	8.6	8.6	8.6
Corporate Profit Tax Accruals as a Percent of Cashflows	20.4	18.8	19.4	19.3	19.4	19.6	19.4	19.7	20.4	20.3	20.5
Energy											
OPEC Price	66.3	20.5	18.8	12.3	9.2	9.2	8.4	7.5	7.1	6.4	6.0
Composite Energy Price	47.4	30.2	22.8	13.3	10.4	11.2	10.8	10.0	9.9	9.4	9.1
Unemployment and Inflation											
Unemployment Rate (percent)	7.6	8.8	8.9	9.0	9.1	8.8	8.8	8.7	8.3	8.1	8.2
Consumer Price Index	13.3	9.1	9.7	7.8	6.6	6.4	6.2	5.8	5.6	5.3	5.2
Core Inflation Rate	8.9	9.1	9.2	9.2	8.5	7.7	6.9	6.2	5.6	5.2	4.8
Shock Inflation Rate	2.3	2.1	1.7	1.0	0.8	0.8	0.8	0.8	0.7	0.6	0.6
Demand Inflation Rate	2.1	-2.1	-1.2	-2.4	-2.7	-2.1	-1.6	-1.1	-0.7	-0.5	-0.3
Investment, Capital Stock, and Output											
Investment Share (percent)	10.6	10.0	9.5	9.2	9.0	8.9	8.8	8.6	8.6	8.6	8.5
Capital Stock	3.0	1.9	1.3	1.1	1.2	1.3	1.4	1.5	1.8	2.0	1.9
Productivity	-2.1	-0.9	1.2	1.0	1.3	1.2	0.8	1.3	1.1	1.1	1.1
Real Wages	-1.7	-0.8	0.3	1.3	1.5	1.2	1.0	1.0	1.1	1.1	0.9
Potential GNP	3.0	2.5	2.4	2.3	2.2	2.0	2.0	2.0	2.0	2.0	1.9

maintaining existing commitments for benefit programs and increases in real military outlays. If this spending path cannot be achieved, as is most probable, personal taxes could be raised or monetary policy tightened to accomplish the same demand reduction.

Monetary policy in this and the subsequent exercises is managed to accommodate the goals of fiscal policy. Real short-term interest rates are maintained at the same values as in the recent DRI trend projection. This interest rate path keeps real short-term rates in the range of -1.12 to 0.56%. Thus, the looser economy is not allowed to produce lower real interest rates which would gradually reverse the demand weakness. The growth in the narrow money supply in Case 1 is 4.1% in the first five years of the decade, considerably less than the 6.1% figure of the last five years, and consistent with the monetarist prescription of an orderly reduction in the long-run money supply target.

The results of this classic and Keynesian exercise of restraining demand management are successful in the sense of achieving the 5% core inflation target, but are a failure in other terms. Unemployment averages 8.9% in the first half of the decade, remaining near the peak of the current recession levels, and can be allowed to improve to only 8.4% in the second five years. In the absence of dramatic innovations in the labor market, the unemployment rates of nonwhite workers would be averaging 16.1% for the decade, the rate for teenagers would be 19.8%. There is no need to spell out the social implications or the political impossibility of pursuing this approach.

The poor results achieved by this method are not entirely due to the sluggish responsiveness of the price level to reduced aggregate demand. An economy operating far below its normal growth path also suffers on the supply side. The share of the gross national product that would be plowed back into nonresidential fixed investment would be held down to 9.0%, below the historical average of 9.8% for the postwar period, and obviously inadequate considering the special investment needs created by the search for domestic energy sources and the need for pollution abatement. Labor supply growth would also be affected somewhat because of the inadequacy of job opportunities for potential new workers and some acceleration of worker retirements. The cumulative loss in the number of hours worked in the low-demand scenario, compared to the recent DRI trend forecast, is 6.8 billion hours, or 4.2% of all hours in 1990. Productivity performance would also be hurt. The low volume of capital formation would fail to equip workers with increasing amounts of capital. A slack economy would cause overhead labor to be used at less than full effectiveness and production processes to operate below the best volumes.

2. *Case 2: Corporate Tax Incentives to Boost Investment*

A core inflation rate of 5% or less can be reached at considerably less social cost if the tax system is used to stimulate capital formation. The core inflation rate depends critically on the productivity trend, which in turn can be improved by equipping workers with more capital and by reducing the average age of the capital stock. In addition, the cost of capital is an important determinant of core inflation, and tax incentives such as depreciation reform or investment tax credits can reduce the average effective cost of capital to business.

The models were used to search for the optimal magnitudes of tax incentives to achieve the 5% core inflation goal. In determining this optimum—keeping in mind that this exercise was conducted without political constraints—it was discovered that tax incentives would be pushed to their maximum point where the corporate income tax would produce virtually no revenue. This result was achieved by shortening economic lives of buildings to 10.2 years and equipment to 5.1 years, and by boosting the investment tax credit to an effective rate of 22.8%. The corporate income tax would be kept at the current rate of 46%, so business would have to engage in the investments in order to receive the benefits of the incentives (Table 8.2).

In actuality, it would not be possible to use the corporate income tax to this extent because of the distribution of profits among companies. With depreciation lives and investment tax credits of the stipulated magnitude, there would be many companies where tax liability was exhausted before incentives could be fully applied, even with carryovers of losses. The deficit would be increased by $40 billion in 1985 and $104 billion in 1990, or an enlargement of 0.9 and 1.6% of GNP. If the extra deficits are unacceptable, monetary policy would have to be eased, which would create some extra inflation.

As a result of the generous investment incentives, the share of the gross national product that is reinvested reaches 11.7% over the next five years and remains high at 11.0% in the 1986-1990 period. In consequence, the capital stock grows by 3.6% in the first half and 2.5% in the second half of the decade. The productivity advance improves to 1.3% for the full interval, which is still below historical performance; various continuing damaging factors, such as demographic changes and high energy costs, prevent full productivity recovery. Potential GNP grows by 2.7% for the decade, which is more than half a point better than its growth under the demand restraint scenario.

Most importantly, the unemployment rate that can be reconciled with the achievement of the anti-inflation objective is improved dramatically. Whereas

Table 8.2
Simulation Results: Corporate Tax Incentives
(Average annual rates of change)

	1980	1981	1982	1983	1984	1985	1986	1987	1988	1989	1990
Policy											
Average Tax Lifetime, Equipment (years)	11.1	5.1	5.1	5.1	5.1	5.1	5.1	5.1	5.1	5.1	5.1
Average Tax Lifetime, Buildings (years)	22.8	10.2	10.2	10.2	10.2	10.2	10.2	10.2	10.2	10.2	10.2
Investment Tax Credit Rate (percent)	8.6	22.8	22.8	22.8	22.8	22.8	22.8	22.8	22.8	22.8	22.8
Corporate Profit Tax Accruals as a Percent of Cashflows	20.4	8.9	8.1	5.5	2.1	0.6	0.1	0.1	1.0	1.1	0.3
Energy											
OPEC Price	66.3	20.8	21.6	17.2	11.8	10.5	10.1	9.0	8.7	8.1	7.4
Composite Energy Price	47.4	30.4	24.8	17.9	13.6	12.8	12.5	11.7	11.6	11.2	10.6
Unemployment and Inflation											
Unemployment Rate (percent)	7.6	8.5	7.9	7.6	7.6	7.5	7.5	7.6	7.2	7.0	7.3
Consumer Price Index	13.3	9.3	10.4	9.4	8.1	7.5	7.1	6.6	6.3	6.2	6.2
Core Inflation Rate	8.9	8.5	7.6	8.0	8.0	7.4	6.8	6.1	5.6	5.2	4.8
Shock Inflation Rate	2.3	2.1	1.9	1.5	1.1	1.0	1.0	0.9	0.8	0.7	0.7
Demand Inflation Rate	2.1	-1.3	0.9	0.0	-0.9	-0.9	-0.7	-0.5	-0.1	0.3	0.7
Investment, Capital Stock, and Output											
Investment Share (percent)	10.6	10.4	11.5	12.5	12.3	11.8	11.6	11.2	11.0	10.8	10.2
Capital Stock	3.0	2.4	3.9	4.5	3.9	3.5	3.1	2.8	2.7	2.5	1.6
Productivity	-2.1	-0.6	1.8	1.3	1.4	2.1	1.5	1.8	1.5	1.3	1.1
Real Wages	-1.7	-0.8	0.0	0.7	1.4	1.7	1.7	1.6	1.6	1.5	1.1
Potential GNP	3.0	2.5	2.5	2.9	3.1	3.0	2.9	2.7	2.6	2.5	2.3

the pure demand policy requires an average unemployment rate of 8.7% for the decade, the corporate tax incentives improve the supply side of the economy sufficiently to make a somewhat less restrictive demand policy possible and to allow unemployment to improve to 7.8% in the first half of the decade and to 7.3% in the second half. Should new approaches to manpower policy be developed and applied, the unemployment goals could be improved, of course. Real government spending rises by a very low 1.0% a year, as demand management has to keep unemployment at a level where it makes a significant disinflationary contribution.

An increase in the investment share of GNP from the historical norm of 9.8% to an estimated 11.7% over the next five years raises the question whether the capital goods industries could meet the volume of demand with which they would be confronted. It has long been recognized in business cycle theory that a high volume of investment will drive up the price of capital goods, thereby lowering the profitability of investment and possibly terminating the investment boom.

The DRI model consists of equations derived from the data of the postwar period, when the investment ratio approached 11% only briefly. Consequently the equations for the prices of capital goods do not fully reflect the potential inflationary effect which would be created by a sizable increase of the investment ratio beyond its historical range. Yet earlier econometric researches by Wilson[1] indicated that machinery prices do respond quite strongly to variations in demand.

A small econometric investigation was undertaken to help define how the model would have to be modified to deal with this particular instance of a simulation exercise going well beyond the range of the historical experience. On the basis of a price equation derived from the record, a simulation rule was entered into the model which assumes that the response of the relative price of machinery with respect to the investment ratio has an elasticity of 0.5; for example, a 10% increase in the investment ratio from say, 10 to 11%, would boost machinery prices by an extra 5%.

3. *Case 3: Corporate Investment Incentives Plus Stability of Energy Prices*

The previous cases carry over the DRI long-term forecast assumptions about OPEC prices. They assume that the real OPEC price, defined in terms of the U.S. price level, will be increasing by 6.1% a year until 1985 and by 2.9%

[1]Thomas A. Wilson, "The Analysis of Machinery Prices," *Study of Employment Growth and Price Levels* (Washington: Joint Economic Committee, 1959).

thereafter. This assumption contributes to a total shock inflation factor of 1.6% a year until 1985 and 1.2% thereafter. This must be overcome by increased weakness in the economy so that demand serves as an offset, or by supply policies which create offsetting cost reductions.

To take the OPEC assumption as given may be political realism, indeed it may even be overoptimistic. But in a study free of the limitations of administrative and political feasibility, it would certainly be inappropriate to take this assumption as if it were engraved in stone. The United States has a variety of options to escape the stranglehold of OPEC. Much has been done: the energy legislation passed in the last two years permits domestic oil and gas prices to gradually move toward world prices to encourage the substitution of other energy sources for oil and to encourage conservation. Progress on mandatory conservation standards for residential buildings and appliances has been slow, and government programs to develop new energy sources such as synthetic fuels are only now entering the beginnings of the development stages. If the United States were to place stability of world energy prices higher on its priority lists, we might well be able to achieve this goal through stronger incentives to domestic oil and gas producers and through policies to permit the greater use of coal or nuclear power.

Without attempting to detail a full energy scenario, a simulation was run in which the real price charged by OPEC is kept constant. This would not imply unchanging real energy prices: the legislated domestic decontrol path is assumed to proceed; the greater substitution of natural gas and coal for oil would imply bigger increases for those fuels; the price level would also keep rising for other reasons. Therefore, the assumption of constant real OPEC prices implies a nominal increase of the composite wholesale price for energy of 12.3% a year for the decade.

These energy price assumptions were combined with the corporate tax incentives of the previous solution. The fiscal policy required to achieve the predetermined goal of a core inflation rate below 5% by 1990 was then calculated by using the model in a series of optimizing runs. The resultant policy is less extreme than in the previous cases, but the trend in real government spending is still held to a modest 2.0% a year.

The conclusions of the resultant simulation are more positive (Table 8.3). With the constant real OPEC price, unemployment can be brought down to an average of 7.2% for the first half of the decade and 6.0% for the period 1986 to 1990. With shock inflation held down, there is a closer coincidence between the "natural" unemployment rate defined by normal search and turnover phenomena in the labor market and the "noninflationary" unemployment rate necessary to avoid a worsening of core inflation.

This solution produces an extraordinarily high rate of investment for the economy. The investment share of GNP is 12.1% for the first half of the

Table 8.3
Simulation Results: Corporate Tax Incentives Plus Constant Real OPEC Price
(Average annual rates of change)

	1980	1981	1982	1983	1984	1985	1986	1987	1988	1989	1990
Policy											
Average Tax Lifetime, Equipment (years)	11.1	5.1	5.1	5.1	5.1	5.1	5.1	5.1	5.1	5.1	5.1
Average Tax Lifetime, Buildings (years)	22.8	10.2	10.2	10.2	10.2	10.2	10.2	10.2	10.2	10.2	10.2
Investment Tax Credit Rate (percent)	8.6	22.8	22.8	22.8	22.8	22.8	22.8	22.8	22.8	22.8	22.8
Corporate Profit Tax Accruals as a Percent of Cashflows	20.4	8.8	8.8	6.8	2.3	0.1	0.0	0.1	0.4	0.1	0.0
Energy											
OPEC Price	66.3	14.1	9.3	8.9	8.1	7.1	6.3	5.8	5.6	5.3	5.0
Composite Energy Price	47.4	27.2	15.7	10.5	10.7	10.6	9.9	9.6	9.9	9.8	9.7
Unemployment and Inflation											
Unemployment Rate (percent)	7.6	8.5	7.6	6.7	6.6	6.6	6.5	6.4	5.9	5.7	5.7
Consumer Price Index	13.3	9.1	9.3	8.4	7.6	7.2	6.7	6.2	6.1	5.9	5.9
Core Inflation Rate	8.9	8.5	7.3	7.5	7.6	7.2	6.5	5.9	5.4	5.1	4.8
Shock Inflation Rate	2.3	1.9	1.5	1.2	1.0	0.9	0.9	0.8	0.8	0.7	0.7
Demand Inflation Rate	2.1	-1.4	0.5	-0.3	-0.9	-0.8	-0.7	-0.5	-0.1	0.1	0.4
Investment, Capital Stock, and Output											
Investment Share (percent)	10.6	10.3	11.6	13.0	13.0	12.5	12.1	11.9	11.8	11.6	11.2
Capital Stock	3.0	2.4	4.2	5.5	5.0	4.2	3.7	3.5	3.4	3.2	2.5
Productivity	-2.1	-0.5	3.0	2.0	0.7	2.0	1.9	2.0	1.6	1.3	1.4
Real Wages	-1.7	-0.6	0.7	1.1	1.5	1.8	1.9	2.0	2.0	2.0	1.8
Potential GNP	3.0	2.5	2.6	3.1	3.5	3.4	3.1	2.8	2.7	2.6	2.5

decade, much beyond historical experience, and 0.4 points higher than in Case 2. For the second five years of the decade, the investment share is 11.7%, an even larger differential compared to Case 2. Once the inflationary pressure from OPEC prices is taken out of the picture, the economy can handle a higher rate of investment while still achieving progress on core inflation. This is a virtuous circle: the higher investment rate reinforces the progress on inflation through its effects on productivity.

The investment program triggered by the tax incentives and fostered by the better energy situation is very large. The 12.1% investment ratio produces a growth in the capital stock of 4.3%, which is higher than thc historical average. This program really would be a "reindustrialization" of the American economy.

The effect on potential real GNP growth is also quite striking. With both strong supply policies and constant real OPEC prices, the growth rate of potential GNP returns to a 3.0% rate in the first half of 1980, the rate which prevailed in the 1950s. The even higher potential growth of the 1960s and early 1970s is not repeated because the growth of the labor force is smaller, technological progress is not fully restored, and the industrial mix of output is not as favorable. In the second half of the 1980s, when labor force growth slows considerably, the growth of potential GNP drops to 2.7%, but that is still sufficiently high to allow the achievement of large real wage gains that match historical performance.

4. Comparisons Summary

Table 8.4 and Charts 8.1 to 8.3 contrast the various solutions. Chart 8.1 shows the three paths of unemployment under the three assumptions, showing that demand policies alone keep unemployment very high, that the tax incentives achieve a somewhat better unemployment path but not one that would be socially desirable. Only the combination of investment stimulus and solution of the OPEC price problem opens up the possibility of reconciling the postulated improvement of the core inflation rate to 5% by 1990 with an average unemployment rate of 6.0% for the second half of the decade.

Chart 8.2 shows that the share of GNP invested in the capital stock is boosted to high rates by historical standards, through the use of the tax incentives, and is boosted even further if the policy can be applied in a context of constant real energy prices.

The increased level of investment converts into major increases in the capital stock. As Chart 8.3 shows, the tax incentives restore the capital stock growth to the historical norm, and if applied in the constant real energy context, boost it further.

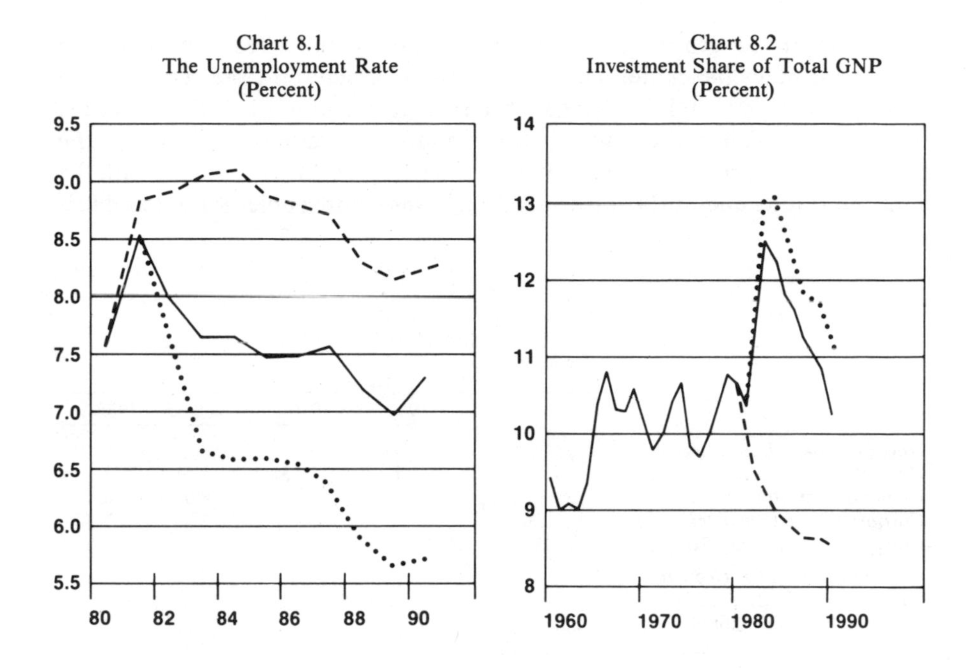

Chart 8.1
The Unemployment Rate
(Percent)

Chart 8.2
Investment Share of Total GNP
(Percent)

Chart 8.3
Change in the Capital Stock
(Percent)

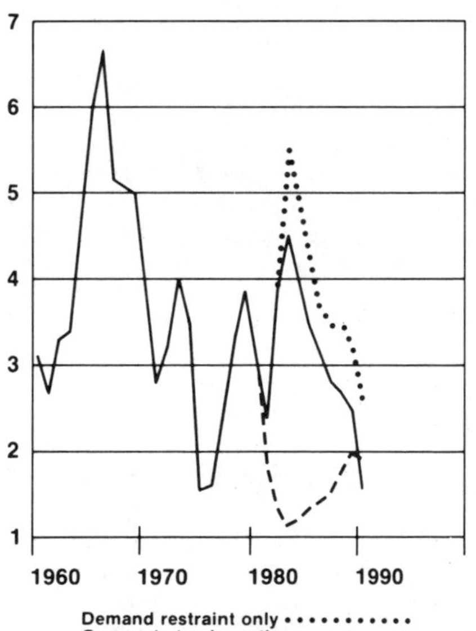

The improved growth of the capital stock creates a restoration of the improvement in the capital-labor ratio that characterized the century-long high productivity trend that has been at the center of U.S. economic development. This improvement in the capital-labor ratio is at the root of the productivity improvement shown in Table 8.4. A fuller summary of the solution results and of the historical data is shown in Tables 8.1-8.3 and 8.5.

Table 8.4
Comparison of Simulations:
Three Strategies to Cut Core Inflation to 5%
(Average annual rates of change)

	1960-70	1970-80	1980-85	1985-90
Unemployment Rate *(percent)*				
History	4.8	6.3		
Demand Restraint Only			8.9	8.4
Corporate Tax Incentives			7.8	7.3
Constant Real Energy Price			7.2	6.0
Potential Real GNP Growth				
History	3.9	3.1		
Demand Restraint Only			2.3	2.0
Corporate Tax Incentives			2.8	2.6
Constant Real Energy Price			3.0	2.7
Productivity				
History	2.5	0.9		
Demand Restraint Only			0.7	1.1
Corporate Tax Incentives			1.2	1.4
Constant Real Energy Price			1.5	1.6
Capital Stock Growth				
History	4.5	3.0		
Demand Restraint Only			1.4	1.7
Corporate Tax Incentives			3.6	2.5
Constant Real Energy Price			4.3	3.3
Investment Share of GNP *(percent)*				
History	9.8	10.2		
Demand Restraint Only			9.3	8.6
Corporate Tax Incentives			11.7	11.0
Constant Real Energy Price			12.1	11.7
Core Inflation				
History	1.7	6.5		
Demand Restraint Only			8.7	5.8
Corporate Tax Incentives			7.9	5.7
Constant Real Energy Price			7.6	5.5

Table 8.5
Summary of Historical Data
(Average annual rates of change)

	1960	1961	1962	1963	1964	1965	1966	1967	1968	1969
Policy										
Average Tax Lifetime, Equipment (years)	15.1	15.1	14.1	13.1	13.1	13.1	13.1	13.1	13.1	13.1
Average Tax Lifetime, Buildings (years)	22.8	22.8	22.8	22.8	22.8	22.8	22.8	22.8	22.8	22.8
Investment Tax Credit Rate (percent)	0.0	0.0	3.3	4.1	4.9	5.8	4.7	4.8	6.1	1.1
Corporate Profit Tax Accruals as a Percent of Cashflows	29.0	28.6	26.8	27.3	26.3	25.7	25.9	24.7	27.1	26.5
Energy										
OPEC Price	NA	0.0	-1.6	-1.1	-5.0	0.0	0.8	4.3	-1.7	7.1
Composite Energy Price	1.0	1.1	-0.5	-0.4	-2.7	1.8	2.5	2.3	-1.1	2.0
Unemployment and Inflation										
Unemployment Rate (percent)	5.5	6.7	5.6	5.6	5.2	4.5	3.8	3.8	3.6	3.5
Consumer Price Index	1.5	1.1	1.2	1.2	1.3	1.6	3.0	2.8	4.2	5.4
Core Inflation Rate	3.1	2.1	1.3	1.1	1.0	0.6	0.9	1.6	1.9	3.0
Shock Inflation Rate	0.1	0.0	0.1	-0.1	-0.2	0.3	0.7	0.0	0.2	0.5
Demand Inflation Rate	-1.6	-1.1	-0.3	0.2	0.6	0.7	1.4	1.2	2.1	1.9
Investment, Capital Stock, and Output										
Investment Share (percent)	9.4	9.0	9.1	9.0	9.4	10.4	10.8	10.3	10.3	10.6
Capital Stock	3.1	2.7	3.3	3.4	4.3	6.0	6.7	5.1	5.0	5.0
Productivity	1.0	2.7	4.2	3.4	3.4	3.3	2.4	1.6	3.2	-0.2
Real Wages	1.4	2.2	1.6	1.3	1.2	1.7	1.4	2.3	2.0	2.1
Potential GNP	3.5	3.5	3.5	3.4	3.4	3.5	4.2	4.9	4.6	4.2

	1970	1971	1972	1973	1974	1975	1976	1977	1978	1979
Policy										
Average Tax Lifetime, Equipment (years)	13.1	11.1	11.1	11.1	11.1	11.1	11.1	11.1	11.1	11.1
Average Tax Lifetime, Buildings (years)	22.8	22.8	22.8	22.8	22.8	22.8	22.8	22.8	22.8	22.8
Investment Tax Credit Rate (percent)	0.0	3.1	5.3	5.6	5.6	8.1	8.1	8.1	8.1	8.4
Corporate Profit Tax Accruals as a Percent of Cashflows	24.1	23.5	22.3	22.7	22.0	20.4	21.6	21.6	22.1	21.3
Energy										
OPEC Price	-1.7	5.0	5.4	23.7	204.9	11.6	-3.0	7.8	0.4	47.6
Composite Energy Price	5.3	8.5	3.0	13.2	55.0	17.7	8.3	13.8	6.7	26.5
Unemployment and Inflation										
Unemployment Rate (percent)	5.0	6.0	5.6	4.9	5.6	8.5	7.7	7.0	6.0	5.8
Consumer Price Index	5.9	4.2	3.3	6.2	11.0	9.1	5.7	6.5	7.7	11.3
Core Inflation Rate	4.1	4.3	4.2	4.4	6.0	7.8	7.7	7.7	8.0	8.2
Shock Inflation Rate	0.4	0.7	0.8	2.9	3.8	1.2	0.6	0.8	1.0	2.2
Demand Inflation Rate	1.4	-0.7	-1.7	-1.1	1.2	0.2	-2.6	-2.0	-1.3	0.8
Investment, Capital Stock, and Output										
Investment Share (percent)	10.2	9.8	10.0	10.4	10.7	9.8	9.7	10.0	10.4	10.8
Capital Stock	3.7	2.8	3.2	4.0	3.5	1.6	1.6	2.3	3.3	3.9
Productivity	0.1	3.1	3.5	1.8	-3.1	2.0	3.5	1.6	0.5	-1.1
Real Wages	2.0	2.6	2.9	0.6	-2.6	0.3	2.1	1.7	1.3	-0.8
Potential GNP	4.1	3.4	3.0	3.0	3.3	3.3	2.6	2.6	2.9	3.3

CHAPTER 9

PRICE EXPECTATIONS AND CORE INFLATION

The core inflation theory is a conceptual structure which combines well-established tools of macroeconomics in a framework suited for an integrated analysis of inflation. In its general formulation, the core inflation theory is neutral with regard to the controversies that divide the field of macroeconomics and can simply be viewed as a particular underpinning to the aggregate supply curve.

The core inflation theory does make a strong assertion on one critical issue, however. To have meaning, core inflation must imply persistence, for if core inflation were highly variable in response to variations in aggregate demand or aggregate supply, there would be no core on which to focus the analysis.

The persistence of core inflation is principally due to the extended process by which the price expectations underlying wage and capital cost trends are formed. The delay in the transmission of demand and supply-shock impulses to actual inflation is defined by the lags in the equations which translate these impulses into actual inflation experience (equations 22-27). These lags average two quarters for the various supply shocks and about three quarters for the demand effect. These are short intervals, short enough to be approximated by models of instantaneous adjustment. But the average lag for price expectations in the wage equation is 10 quarters and in the interest rate equation it is six quarters, thereby creating very slow adjustment processes.

Before accepting the generally pessimistic conclusions of the core inflation analysis, it is necessary to examine more closely the dynamic processes by which expectations are formed. In this chapter, the empirical underpinnings of this critical element in the core inflation theory are examined through a series of statistical tests of the specifications of the critical wage and interest rate equations.

1. The Rational Expectations Viewpoint

The theory of rational expectations invented by Muth[1] and developed by Lucas[2] is consistent with the core inflation theory in some versions and quite contradictory to it in others. The rational expectations hypothesis maintains that economic agents properly consider the available information in making decisions, and that these decisions will, on the average, be free of systematic forecasting bias. In the case of prices, where the theory has been most commonly applied, this hypothesis asserts that price expectations will be formed on the basis of a mental model which correctly derives the long-term inflation outlook from historical observations and assumptions about monetary policy. Of course, inflation contains an unpredictable element, but under rational expectations the expected value of a probability distribution of future prices would be correct.

The empirical implementation of the Core Inflation Model is consistent with this "weak" version of the rational expectations theory. As the equation displayed in Table 9.1 shows, the coefficients on the price expectations terms in the DRI model's wage equation sum to 0.84, sufficiently close to unity not to be significantly different. Price expectations in the long-term interest rate equation (Table 9.4), the other important testing ground of the rational expectations assumption, also show a value close to unity. Thus, at this level of specificity, the core inflation theory is consistent with the rational expectations viewpoint.

The widely heralded and debated policy conclusions of the rational expectations theory depend upon a stronger set of assumptions, however. If individuals anticipate the inflationary results of policy correctly, they would sharply reduce, and in a limiting case fully defeat, the intended results of policy. Easier money would immediately produce higher inflation and no change in output or unemployment. This reasoning requires instant learning, i.e., that expectations are not only free of bias, but that they are formed and acted on immediately upon receipt of new information. This is the "strong" rational expectations hypothesis.

Under this "strong" rational expectations viewpoint, the core inflation theory could not be correct. The gradual determination of the core inflation rate depends upon the existence of slow learning processes by which price expectations are formed. Thus, the smoothness and persistence of the

[1]John F. Muth, "Rational Expectations and the Theory of Price Movements," *Econometrica,* July 1961, pp. 315-335.

[2]R.E. Lucas, Jr., "Econometric Policy Evaluation, A Critique," in Karl Brunner and Allan H. Meltzer, eds., *The Phillips Curve and Labor Markets* (Amsterdam: North-Holland Publishing Co., 1976), pp. 19-46; and R.J. Gordon, "Can Econometric Policy Evaluation be Salvaged? A Comment," *ibid.,* pp. 47-61.

Table 9.1
Wage Equation in the DRI Model

Ordinary Least Squares

Quarterly (1956:1 to 1979:1)—93 Observations
Dependent Variable: 400*log(JAHEADJEA/JAHEADJEA(-1))

	Coefficient	Standard error	t-Stat	Independent variable
1)	0.206108	0.06456	3.192	100*log(PC(-1)/PC/(-5))
2)	0.629963	0.07306	8.623	PCEXP85
3)	11.1579	0.6999	15.94	1/(RU-RUADJ)
4)				PDL(%MINWAGE400,1,4,FAR)
/0.........	0.0102843	0.003743		
/1.........	0.00771322	0.002808		
/2.........	0.00514215	0.001872		
/3.........	0.00257107	0.0009359		
Sum.......	0.0257107	0.009359	2.747	
Average ...	1.00000	0.0	NC	
5)	0.605270	0.2026	2.988	DGPOST
6)	2.13063	0.5253	4.056	ALTP1
7)	-2.25031	0.7629	-2.950	DMY641

R-Bar squared: 0.8573
F-statistic (7,86): 764.5
Durbin-Watson statistic: 1.4632
Sum of squared residuals: 47.34
Standard error of the regression: 0.7419 Normalized: 0.1393

JAHEADJEA is the index of hourly earnings of private nonfarm production workers,
PC is the implicit price deflator for personal consumption expenditures,
PCEXP85 is the expected rate of inflation for personal expenditures deflator (numerals indicate persistence factor),
RU is the unemployment rate for all civilian workers,
RUADJ is the adjustment to the full-employment unemployment rate,
%MINWAGE400 is the logarithmic first difference of MINWAGE,
DGPOST is the guidepost dummy,
ALTP1 is a dummy variable for Phase 1 of the Nixon Controls Program,
DMY641 is the dummy for the break in the JAHEADJEA series, apparent data error.

inflation expectations build-up is created by the slow learning processes by which individuals extract additional information from actual economic data, letting several years of experience accumulate before changing their fundamental judgment on the inflation outlook.

The same disagreement applies to ex ante calculations about the future of core inflation. If "strong" rational expectations apply, the announcement of a changed economic policy regime, such as the adoption of monetarist rules with modest targets, would be processed through the mental models in the minds of economic agents and would result in an immediate lowering of inflation expectations. Long-term interest rates would therefore fall and wage claims would decline drastically, reducing core inflation upon receipt of the announcement. Even if policy announcements lack credibility with a public insisting on actual experience, a quick learning process might still produce a close approximation to the "strong" rational expectations result. Tight money would lower aggregate demand and reduce sensitive commodity prices to produce reductions in the short-term inflation record. Demand effects might still take two or three quarters to affect the price indexes, but this observed information would then be quickly processed into lower inflation expectations.

The key factual and theoretical issue, therefore, dividing the "strong" rational expectations viewpoint from the core inflation approach is the assumption about the speed of learning of households and businesses from actual experience or from policy announcements. If learning processes are rapid, the rewards for anti-inflationary demand policies would be great, and the costs in terms of lost output and unemployment would be small. On the other hand, if the kinds of equations built into the DRI model, embodying gradual learning processes, describe the empirical reality, then core inflation is stubborn indeed, and the progress that could be achieved by politically plausible demand policies, including the monetarist recipe of an orderly reduction of money growth, would be disappointingly small.

2. Price Expectations in the Wage Equation: Has Learning Speeded Up?

Traditional wage equations rely on extended distributed lags to define the price expectations which define wage claims. An earlier paper using data through 1976 tested alternative equations with different expectations mechanisms. Gradual learning from actual experience rather than quick learning from recent data about prices or money proved to be the better explanation of the data.[3]

One might conjecture that the period of extreme inflation has accelerated the learning processes by which price expectations are formed. If learning has quickened, then the equations based on the statistical record of a much longer postwar interval would not be representative of conditions in the future and would portray too pessimistic a prospect. If price expectations adapt more quickly now than they did in the past, the rate of wage increase would retreat more rapidly in response to the better price performance that could be created by weak demand and favorable shock experience, and the labor cost element of core inflation would show bigger improvement.

[3]Otto Eckstein, "Economic Theory and Econometric Models," Paper presented to Ann Arbor Conference on Econometric Models, August 1978, (to be published in the Conference volume).

What has happened to price expectations of workers and employees during the last six years of rapid inflation? To begin to answer this question, a series of statistical tests have been performed using wage equations which follow the standard formulation of the literature. The results are quite surprising, both for the assessment of the core inflation analysis and for the strong version of the rational expectations theory.

The wage equation in the DRI model, shown in Table 9.1, relies on the inverse of a demography-corrected national unemployment rate, proxy variables for the period of intense guidepost policy in the mid-1960s and the wage-price controls of 1971-74, as well as a dummy variable for the first quarter of 1964 when there appears to have been a major measurement error in the official data. The price expectations factor in the wage equation is modeled through two variables: expectations based on the short-term price experience of the preceding four quarters with a coefficient of .21, and expectations based on a longer experience using a decay factor of .15, with a coefficient of .63. The sum of the price coefficients, .84, is sufficiently close to unity to be consistent with rational expectations.

While this is an equation with good statistical properties, it has a systematic bias beginning in 1974. The equation overpredicts wage changes, indicating that, as a first approximation, the reaction of wages to prices has become weaker, not stronger, since the OPEC burst of energy inflation.

A confirming test of this initial finding is obtained by refitting the equation to the period 1956-73 and testing that equation for the succeeding years. The shift in wage behavior is demonstrated more strongly by this test. The equation has total price coefficients of 1.1, still not significantly higher than the rational expectations value of unity, but one which could easily lead to explosive wage-price behavior. Fitting the equation to the highly unstable and brief period 1974-79 produces low statistical quality and erratic coefficients. The short-term price expectations variable, the variable that would indicate a quicker learning process, becomes statistically insignificant and even takes on the wrong sign. Apparently, workers, union leaders, and employers recognized that the series of inflation shocks associated with food and energy were transitory and therefore likely to be reversed. This is consistent with the behavior observed in long-term historical studies going back to the nineteenth century, in which a negative elasticity of expectations was found, i.e., above-average rates of inflation were likely to be soon reversed as crops might improve or the economy thrown into recession.[4]

The statistically significant break in the economic structure of wage determination that occurred in 1974 calls for a more elaborate reexamination

[4]Otto Eckstein and James Girola, "Long-Term Properties of the Price-Wage Mechanism in the United States, 1891 to 1977," *Review of Economics and Statistics*, August 1978, pp. 323-333.

of the equation. Both the principal variables and the lag structures defining expectations require another empirical review.

The initial econometric studies of wages for the U.S. found the profitability of industry to be a significant explanatory variable,[5] following the ideas of Dunlop[6] which emphasized product market conditions and ability-to-pay as important wage determinants. The econometric studies of the late 1960s and the early 1970s saw the profit variables disappear from significance. However, regressions covering the entire time span from 1956 to 1979 show a significant return of the profit variable. It is strongest in the form of the change in the economy-wide change in margins, suggesting that profits add a cyclical element to wage behavior, based on ability-to-pay and perhaps the potential profit loss of strikes.

The second traditional variable that was tested was the burden of personal taxation. An earlier study[7] found that an increase in the burden of the personal income and payroll taxes was shifted forward into higher wages, albeit only temporarily. The large increases in the tax burden of recent years could, one might conjecture, be shifted forward into higher wages. The surprise in recent wages is the smallness of the increases, however. Regression results show the tax burden variable not to be significant, and indeed to have the wrong sign.

While none of the variables tested account for the downshifting of the wage equation after 1973, the equation accepts a dummy to reflect a change in the constant of considerable size, though of marginal statistical significance. A typical equation incorporating the downshift dummy and the profit variable is shown in Table 9.2.

The changing role of short-term price expectations is shown dramatically in the equation. It allows the coefficient on the one-year price term to vary between the intervals 1956-73 and 1974-80:1. In the earlier period, the short-term price variable takes a coefficient of .70, producing a total price effect of 1.13 when combined with the long-term price effect. While too large, the effect is less than one standard deviation from unity. In the period after 1973, the short-term price effect drops to .20, making for a total price effect of .63, which is statistically different from unity.

Various hypotheses can be advanced for the downshift. International trade is representing an increasing fraction of the gross national product and tariff and other trade barriers have declined. With our principal competitors following more successful anti-inflation policies and experiencing smaller

[5]Otto Eckstein and Thomas A. Wilson, "The Determination of Money Wages in American Industry," *The Quarterly Journal of Economics,* 76, August 1962, pp. 379-414.

[6]John T. Dunlop, *Wage Determination Under Trade Unions,* (New York: Macmillan & Co., Ltd.,1944), p. 125.

[7]Otto Eckstein and Roger Brinner, "The Inflation Process in the United States," Study prepared for the Joint Economic Committee, February 22, 1972 (Washington: U.S. Government Printing Office), pp. 17-18.

Table 9.2
Wage Equation Allowing for Structural Changes After 1973

Ordinary Least Squares
Quarterly (1956:1 to 1980:1)—97 Observations
Dependent Variable: 400*log(JAHEADJEA/JAHEADJEA(-1))

	Coefficient	Standard error	t-Stat	Independent variable
	1.74533	1.441	1.212	Constant
1)	7.03956	1.719	4.095	1/(RU-RUADJ)
2)	....		....	PDL(%MINWAGE400,1,4,FAR)
/0.........	0.0190321	0.004224		
/1.........	0.0142741	0.003168		
/2.........	0.00951605	0.002112		
/3.........	0.00475803	0.001056		
Sum.......	0.0475803	0.01056	4.505	
Average ...	1.00000	0.0	NC	
3)	0.300417	0.2298	1.307	DGPOST
4)	2.61378	0.6334	4.126	ALTP1
5)	-2.86210	0.7258	-3.943	DMY641
6)	0.0123280	0.003356	3.674	400*log(ZA%GNP/ZA%GNP(-1))
7)	0.703921	0.1330	5.292	DMYPRE74*100* log(PC(-1)/PC(-5))
8)	0.200955	0.07815	2.571	(1-DMYPRE74)*100* log(PC(-1)/PC(-5))
9)	-1.69192	1.158	-1.460	DMYPRE74
10)	0.426870	0.1634	2.612	PCEXP86

R-Bar squared: 0.8795
F-statistic (10,86): 71.05
Durbin-Watson statistic: 1.7759
Sum of squared residuals: 41.54
Standard error of the regression: 0.6950 Normalized: 0.1278

JAHEADJEA is the index of hourly earnings of private nonfarm production workers,
RU is the unemployment rate for all civilian workers,
RUADJ is the adjustment to the full-employment unemployment rate,
%MINWAGE400 is the logarithmic first difference of MINWAGE,
DGPOST is the guidepost dummy,
ALTP1 is a dummy variable for Phase 1 of the Nixon Controls Program,
DMY641 is a dummy for the break in the JAHEADJEA series, apparent data error,
ZA%GNP is aftertax profits as a percentage of GNP,
DMYPRE74 is a dummy set at zero until 1973, unity thereafter,
PC is the implicit price deflator for personal consumption expenditures,
PCEXP86 is the expected rate of inflation for the personal expenditures deflator (numerals indicate persistence factor).

wage increases, logic would dictate that there would be some effect on wages in the United States so long as the exchange rates are not fully flexible. Arguing against this hypothesis is the astonishing relative wage behavior in the United States in which the industries most directly damaged by international trade are continuing to show wage increases far above the national average.

Another hypothesis which might explain the downshift is the decline of unionization in the private sector, and particularly the extraordinary focus of economic growth in the "Sunbelt," where unions are weak. Because this shift has been continuing throughout these years at a fairly regular pattern, it is not possible to find a statistically significant effect from aggregate time series data but it may still be the basic cause.

Recent years have also seen an extraordinary expansion of the supply of labor because of the increased participation of women. Equal employment opportunity legislation may also have raised competitiveness in various occupations. Increased competition from nonwhites and women could be serving as a dampening effect on wage increases.

Finally, the downshift of nominal wages since 1973 may perhaps be explained by a realistic perception by workers and union leaders that high energy prices have seriously damaged the economy's productivity performance and required the massive transfer of real income to the oil producers. Whereas wage determination, whether through collective bargaining or market mechanisms, may preserve equilibrium in the distribution of income between labor and capital in the United States, it may also reflect a willingness to pay the price of costly foreign energy at the expense of real purchasing power. This viewpoint would be consistent both with the downshift of wages as well as the statistical observation that wages have responded only weakly to the energy-dominated short-run price changes since 1973.

3. Another Test of the Speed of Formation of Price Expectations

The speed of learning can also be assessed by varying the lag structure and observing the effect on the statistical quality of the equation.

Table 9.3 summarizes a set of regressions in which the model equation is tested with alternative speeds of learning for long-term price expectations. The strongest statistical results are achieved with a relatively slow learning process, with a decay factor of .17—or a persistence factor of .83—which implies a mean lag of 9.8 quarters. While the response of R-bar squared to the decay factor is fairly flat over a broad range, it is evident that the statistical quality does deteriorate substantially when the decay factor reaches .30, putting the mean lag at five quarters. The long-term expectations appear to be formed over an interval considerably longer than a year. Given the three-year length of many collective bargaining agreements and the usual annual wage review of unorganized workers, such lags are not surprising. It is also striking that the price coefficients decline as the lags are shortened: if learning is modeled to be quicker, it is less complete.

Table 9.3
Price Expectations in the Wage Equation

Decay Factor	Mean Lag in Quarters	R-bar Squared	Price Coefficient	Durbin-Watson Data
.05	38.0	.821	.883	1.20
.10	18.0	.850	.830	1.37
.15	11.3	.860	.775	1.46
.17	9.8	.861	.752	1.46
.20	8.0	.860	.738	1.45
.25	6.0	.853	.706	1.39
.30	4.7	.843	.675	1.32
.35	3.7	.835	.649	1.28
.40	3.0	.828	.625	1.25

4. Conclusion on Wages

Wage behavior has changed since 1973 in ways that contradict the strong version of the rational expectations hypothesis and support the core inflation theory. While the downshift of the wage relations may be explained by increased competitiveness in the labor market, reduced productivity growth, or the recognition that OPEC is enforcing real income cuts on the economy, it still is the opposite of an increased sensitivity of wages to accelerating inflation. More importantly from the theoretical point of view, the near-disappearance of the short-term price effect on wages suggests that learning has become slower, that workers are finding it more difficult to extract correct price expectations from increasingly large and volatile price movements that they are observing. In the particular formulation found to be the optimum equation in the current exercise, the total price effect also seems to have fallen out of the statistical zone that could not be distinguished from unity, i.e., the equation is not even consistent with the weak version of rational expectations. That result is far more tentative and could be upset by other formulations. The diminished sensitivity of wages to prices is so strongly revealed in the data, however, that it is hard to envisage how additional statistical work could upset it. The wage data are not kind to the strong rational expectations viewpoint. There is a stubborn core to inflation, at least on the wage side.

5. Price Expectations for Long-Term Interest Rates

A similar test was conducted to explore the speed of learning of participants in the bond market. The DRI model equation for new, top quality corporate bonds, which is shown in Table 9.4, depends principally on price expectations,

Table 9.4
Bond New Issue Rate Equation in DRI Model

Ordinary Least Squares

Quarterly (1954:1 to 1979:3)—103 Observations
Dependent Variable: RMMBCNEWNS

	Coefficient	Standard error	T-Stat	Independent variable
	-13.3067	1.283	-10.38	Constant
1)	-5.19846	0.8645	-6.013	log((RESFRBNB+CURR+RRADJ)/(PGNP*N)
2)	0.147057	0.06930	2.122	RMDIFF
3)	0.268448	0.1393	1.927	DMYVIET
4)	6.69214	0.5144	13.01	log(GNP72/N)
5)	3.86513	3.468	1.115	log((NFCBONDS/(PGNP*N))/(NFCBONDS(-1)/(PGNP(-1)*N(-1))))
6)	0.431036	0.07637	5.644	RMAAAGSLNS(-1)
7)	-17.5255	6.305	-2.779	log(((LIRES-LIPL)/(PGNP*N))/((LIRES(-1)-LIPL(-1))/(PGNP(-1)*N(-1))))
8)	0.793035	0.1209	6.557	PCEXP79
9)	-0.0560179	0.01064	-5.265	PCEXP79*(RU+RU(-1)+RU(-2)+RU(-3))/4
10)	0.00627718	0.001982	3.167	JS&PEXP34
11)				PDL(LETRMMBCNEWNS,1,12,FAR)
/0.........	-5.81348	1.353	-4.296	
/1.........	-5.32902	1.240	-4.296	
/2.........	-4.84456	1.128	-4.296	
/3.........	-4.36011	1.015	-4.296	
/4.........	-3.87565	0.9021	-4.296	
/5.........	-3.39119	0.7894	-4.296	
/6.........	-2.90674	0.6766	-4.296	
/7.........	-2.42228	0.5638	-4.296	
/8.........	-1.93783	0.4511	-4.296	
/9.........	-1.45337	0.3383	-4.296	
/10........	-0.968913	0.2255	-4.296	
/11........	-0.484456	0.1128	-4.296	
Sum.......	-37.7876	8.796	-4.296	
Average ...	3.66667	0.0	NC	

R-Bar squared: 0.9877
F-statistic (11,91): 748.5
Durbin-Watson statistic: 1.8875
Sum of squared residuals: 4.714
Standard error of the regression: 0.2276 Normalized: 0.03760

RMMBCNEWNS is the average yield on new issues of high-grade corporate bonds,
RESFRBNB is nonborrowed reserves of Federal Reserve member banks,
CURR is the currency component of the money supply,
RRADJ is the reserve adjustment for changes in reserve requirements since 1959,
PGNP is the implicit price deflator for gross national product,
N is the total population including Armed Forces overseas,
RMDIFF is a measure of bank liquidity,

DMYVIET is a dummy for the Vietnam war,
GNP72 is gross national product in 1972 dollars,
NFCBONDS is nonfinancial corporate bonds,
RMAAAGSLNS is tax exempt bonds,
LIRES is life insurance reserves outstanding,
LIPL is life insurance policy loans outstanding,
PCEXP79 is the expected rate of inflation for the personal expenditures deflator (numerals indicate persistence factor),
RU is the unemployment rate for all civilian workers,
JS&PEXP34 is the expectations variable for Standard & Poor's stock price index,
LETRMMBCNEWNS is the growth of the real per capita monetary base.

along with a liquidity measure, defined as the real per capita monetary base in relation to per capita real GNP. Other variables are the returns on competing investment media including common stocks and tax-exempt securities, and dummies to represent the shocks to the bond market that occurred during the Vietnam War. A secondary price expectations variable is corrected by the unemployment rate, to indicate that market participants interpret inflation differently if unemployment is abnormally high or low.

Table 9.5 summarizes the alternative regressions run with different decay factors in price expectations. It can be seen that the best equation, as judged by the standard statistical criteria of R-bar squared and the Durbin-Watson statistic, has a decay factor of .24, implying an average lag of 6.3 quarters. The variation in the results is very slight as the decay factor varies from .20 to .30, a range spanning lags from 8.0 to 4.7 quarters. However, as the average lag shrinks below six quarters, the price coefficient drops and becomes significantly smaller than unity. Thus, in order to keep the price coefficient within two standard deviations of the value of unity required by rational expectations, the average lag must be upward of six quarters. Insistence on quicker learning formulations, with larger decay factors and shorter lags, produces a less complete learning process, in which the price coefficient is nearer one-half than 1.0. Indeed, as the lags are shortened still further, the price coefficient shrinks to even smaller values as other variables partially replace price expectations as explanatory variables.

While the exploration of price expectations in the long-term interest rate equation has not been as thorough as the exercise for the wage equation by confining itself strictly to the formulation in the current DRI model, the results are similar. The average lag is on the order of six quarters, which is sufficiently long that an improvement in the actual inflation rate impacts the capital cost component of core inflation only very gradually. The participants in the bond market seem to form their price expectations almost as gradually from actual experience as the participants in the labor market.

Table 9.5
Price Expectations in the
Long-Term Interest Rate Equation

Decay Factor	Average Lag in Quarters	R-bar Squared	Price Coefficient	Durbin-Watson Statistic
.10	18.0	.9800	.76	1.25
.20	8.0	.9865	.79	1.66
.21	7.5	.9871	.81	1.71
.24	6.3	.9881	.79	1.79
.30	4.7	.9879	.58	1.72
.35	3.7	.9873	.45	1.65
.45	2.4	.9863	.31	1.59
.50	2.0	.9860	.27	1.59

6. Change in Regime?

The preceding statistical tests are confined to the postwar record of the United States, decades of continuity of the economic system. The rational expectations school finds hope and comfort in the proposition that inflationary price expectations could be wiped from people's minds through adoption of a new economic regime. Certainly there are circumstances in which the public is convinced that the economic order is changed and that the historical record is not a useful source of information about future performance. Political revolutions, both of the right and left, particularly the replacement of democracy with dictatorships, usually make the collective memory irrelevant and provide the opportunity to start over in developing price expectations. The hyperinflations of the past have all ended, one way or another, usually with a crash and drastic monetary reform.[8]

For the United States, the pertinent question is whether a sufficientchange in regime is possible. The rational expectations school believes that adoption of a sufficiently stringent monetarist rule will suffice, that the public need only be persuaded that future money growth will be rigidly limited, either to be brought down gradually in an orderly way or, in the more drastic version, to be brought down to near-zero in one expectations-shattering step.

Empirical evidence to evaluate this proposition is very limited, and so it cannot be ruled out with certitude. But there have been three minor changes of regime in the last decade which are worth a quick glance. The first episode is the very partial adoption of monetarism in February 1970 when Dr. Arthur F.

[8]See Thomas J. Sargent, "The Ends of Four Big Inflations," NBER Working Paper, October 1980, for an analysis of the ends of hyperinflation.

Burns became Chairman of the Federal Reserve Board. Because the initial move under the new approach was one of easing, little benefit was to be expected for price expectations, and indeed there seems to have been none.

The second change of regime was the imposition of a wage-price freeze by President Nixon in August 1971. This policy was largely justified as an attempt to improve expectations. Yet when the episode was over, there was little or no net gain in inflation results, and price expectations were affected no more and no less by the interval of temporarily better price results than by any other historical observations.[9] This episode leaves no doubt that brief periods of price controls are not a sufficient change of regime.

Finally, the Federal Reserve adopted a stricter monetarist policy in October 1979 which comes fairly close to the prescription of the rational expectations school. Control of the monetary aggregates was made the dominant policy objective, and gradual deceleration of money growth was promised. While doubts remained whether policy would sacrifice all other goals to this objective, the initial policies were very severe, triggering the sharpest decline in economic activity since the end of World War II, followed by a quick upswing of interest rates in the earliest stages of recovery, all designed to complete a successful first year of the new monetary regime.

Despite these changes, no improvement in price expectations resulted, and there surely was no break in the learning pattern. The new policy initially drove interest rates up sharply as fear of a liquidity shortage swamped any possible price expectations benefits. Thereafter, interest rates returned to their usual quantitative behavior, settling near their normal real levels based on slow learning, and varying with liquidity, flows of funds, and observed money supply data interpreted as guides to coming policies.

7. *Conclusion*

Controversy over the speed of learning about inflation will continue for years because the resolution of this question has such strong implications for the central controversy of macroeconomics today, the nature of the response of the economy to monetary and fiscal policies. If the price response is slow, as the present study indicates, classic restraint produces high and sustained unemployment before inflation is defeated; if the response is quick, the social cost of the demand-restraint solution is small. Individuals seem to form their

[9]See Robert J. Gordon, "The Impact of Aggregate Demand on Prices," Brookings Economic Papers, 1975:3, pp. 613-662; and Otto Eckstein, *The Great Recession,* (Amsterdam: North-Holland Publishing Co., 1978), pp. 49-60 and 160-64.

price expectations by a gradual learning process and find it particularly difficult to learn from highly unstable data.

Once the slowness of learning is acknowledged, the rest of the core inflation theory easily falls into place: gradually formed price expectations mean persistent core inflation because they imply a strong continuity of wages and interest rates. If the costs of labor and capital cannot be made to respond quickly, then much of the burden of adjustment to policies and shocks falls on the real variables, on output, employment, and unemployment.

CHAPTER 10

SUPPLY IN THE DRI QUARTERLY ECONOMETRIC MODEL OF THE U.S. ECONOMY

The core inflation analysis focusses on the supply-side of the economy. The core rate is synonymous with the increase in the aggregate factor supply price. While the prices of labor and capital are set in the two factor markets and are mainly determined by expectations, the productivity factor is derived from the aggregate production function. For tax policy to affect core inflation it must affect expectations and factor costs, or it must affect factor supplies and productivity. An assessment of the underpinnings of the core inflation analysis therefore requires a discussion of the supply-side of the DRI model used for the analysis.

1. Return of Supply Economics

While supply antedates demand in the history of economic thought starting with the work of Adam Smith[1] and stretching to John Stuart Mill,[2] and always retained at least an equal share with demand in the field of microeconomics, it must be acknowledged that demand overshadowed supply in macroeconomic analysis since the Great Depression and the rise of Keynesian national income analysis.[3] In the serious academic literature, however, supply theory regained prominence rather quickly: the path-breaking growth model of R.F. Harrod[4] analyzed, at least in a primitive way, the need to match the growth of aggregate supply and aggregate demand, and the model of Domar[5] introduced Harrod's ideas into the American literature.

[1]Adam Smith, *Wealth of Nations,* 1776, Modern Library Edition (New York: Random House, 1937).
[2]John Stuart Mill, *Principles of Political Economy* (London, 1848).
[3]John Maynard Keynes, *The General Theory of Employment, Interest, and Money* (New York: Macmillan & Co., Ltd., 1936).
[4]R.F. Harrod, "Essay in Dynamic Theory," *Economic Journal,* 1939.
[5]Evsey Domar, "Capital Expansion, Rate of Growth, and Employment," *Econometrica,* April 1946, pp. 137-147.

The modern theory of growth initiated by Solow[6] revived the aggregate production function of Cobb-Douglas, showed its central role in the economy, and launched the search for better aggregate production functions. Even in the Keynesian years, the input-output analysis of Wassily Leontief[7] offered theoretical and empirical models which had a production and supply focus. Kendrick's[8] and Denison's[9] analyses of growth and productivity, Schultz'[10] and Becker's[11] work on human capital, and the large body of writings by Griliches, Jorgenson, Mansfield, and many other scholars made the 1950s and 1960s the most fertile decades for the scientific study of the supply-side of the economy.

However, this body of work had little impact on the macroeconomics used for policy. Aggregate demand seemed to be the determining factor of output and the price level in the postwar decades. The growth of aggregate supply could be modelled adequately by the simplest productivity calculations, multiplying labor supply by a productivity trend derived by historical extrapolation. Okun's law,[12] which was based at least implicitly on these productivity projections, seemed perfectly adequate to identify the gap between aggregate demand and aggregate supply, to estimate the unemployment rate, and to help set the gauges for fiscal policy. The great tax cut of 1964 was derived from Okun's law estimates of the "gap" divided by accepted estimates of the multiplier on personal tax cuts. Even in the immediate years after 1964, when demand became excessive and highly sophisticated methods for estimating aggregate production functions were available, the simpler methods seemed to suffice: taxes should have been higher, but it was not a shortcoming of economic analysis that made policy wrong.

The large-scale econometric models which began to take over the tasks of policy analysis in the early 1970s did contain some supply-side elements: aggregate production functions, sophisticated equations for investment and capital stocks, detailed measures of industrial production and capacity, input-output tables, and equations for the availability of finance. But the production functions used were still relatively simple and unresponsive,

[6]Robert M. Solow, "A Contribution to the Theory of Economic Growth," *Quarterly Journal of Economics,* February 1956, pp. 65-94.

[7]Wassily W. Leontief, *The Structure of American Economy, 1919-1939* (New York: Oxford University Press, 1941).

[8]John W. Kendrick, *Productivity Trends in the United States* (Princeton: Princeton University Press, 1961).

[9]Edward F. Denison, *The Sources of Economic Growth in the United States and the Alternatives Before Us,* Supplementary Paper 13 (New York: Committee for Economic Development, 1962).

[10]Theodore W. Schultz, "Investment in Human Capital," *American Economic Review,* March 1961, pp. 1-17.

[11]Gary S. Becker, *Human Capital* (Washington: National Bureau of Economic Research, 1964).

[12]Arthur M. Okun, "Potential GNP: Its Measurement and Significance," *Proceedings of the Economic Statistics Section of the American Statistical Association, (Washington:* 1962).

following the Cobb-Douglas tradition in which the link of investment to potential output is relatively weak and slow, and the technology residual is exogenous and impervious to policy. Energy was not in the picture, of course.

The decade of the 1970s posed different and increasingly serious challenges to macroeconomic analysis. The worldwide boom of 1971-73 produced acute shortages of capacity in the materials-producing industries even though aggregate measures did not signal shortages. The OPEC revolution of 1973 and the subsequent surges of world oil prices had devastating effects on the economic performance of the entire industrial world. The end of productivity growth in 1973 and the resultant explosion of employment repealed Okun's law or any simple calculation of the productivity trend.

The new circumstances make the growth of potential output, or aggregate supply, one of the two or three most critical variables for the economy. Once the potential GNP trend is no longer a *deus ex machina* that drives the economy forward regardless of short-term policies or circumstances, the variables that determine the increase of potential again become the center of attention, as they had been through most of history. What are the critical determinants of the supplies of the factors of production? How do they combine to determine aggregate productivity? And how do policies affect them? These are the supply-side issues that need to be modeled.

2. Supply Features of the DRI Model

While the DRI model has long contained major aspects of the supply side of the economy, the 1980 version includes various new elements designed to have the model benefit from the growing body of scientific work on this topic. These innovations include some tax effects in the equations for the supply of labor and potential output and a more elaborate and more quickly adjusting equation for the determination of aggregate potential, as well as the inclusion of the rental price of capital in the equations for the individual wholesale prices of the input-output-based stage-of-processing sector.

DRI has also revised its simulation methodology for supply-oriented policies in order to more clearly distinguish between the traditional Keynesian multipliers and the newer supply multipliers. In the past, DRI model solutions testing fiscal policies have usually used an unchanged pattern of nonborrowed bank reserves as the definition of a "neutral" monetary policy. As a result, a large part of the initial effect of a supply-based tax change was to create extra activity through the Keynesian multiplier before the supply effects could be felt. While this made policies look very favorable in terms of the creation of employment and activity, it blurred the effects on inflation and supply because the extra stimulus produced a tighter economy. DRI is now using a definition of "neutral" monetary policy based on unchanged real short-term interest rates. The identification of fiscal policy effects is now based on the "differential incidence" viewpoint,[13] with offsetting changes in government expenditures or personal taxes introduced to keep the aggregate unemployment rate unchanged. These policy definitions allow a clearer distinction between aggregate supply and aggregate demand effects. This is not to foreclose the policy choice for aggregate demand: the government can decide to divide the benefits of supply policies between higher real activity and lessened inflation. But thc method leaves a clearer set of analytical conclusions by isolating the supply effects.

The changes in the model create somewhat stronger supply effects than earlier versions but do not turn the conclusions upside-down. The economy's ability to produce responds more positively to tax incentive changes. The magnitudes are limited, and even with a more quickly responding measure of potential, the effects are slow and require much patience. Unless carefully offset by tighter money or fiscal moves, supply-oriented tax cuts initially boost demand more than supply, and thereby initially make inflation worse. The reductions of actual and core inflation come later, and indeed do not come at all without some reinforcing demand management. The federal deficit is enlarged by the tax moves unless they are fully offset by reduced spending or increases of other taxes.

While realistic estimates of supply effects leave no room for miracles, they do indicate major opportunities for restoring productivity performance and partial recovery of long-term growth rates toward the historical norm. The decline in productivity performance is due to a considerable extent to the lack of improvement of the capital-labor ratio and to reduced investment in research and development. The capital stock is aging excessively and is using too much energy for current prices. Supply policies can reverse these factors.

The model also focusses on the imbalance between the supply of labor and the supply of industrial capacity. The changed historical relationship between the utilization rates of basic industries and national unemployment produces extra inflation. The deterioration of delivery conditions in industrial markets is measured by the critical vendor performance measure of the model and affects monetary policies and prices. High utilization rates also directly create inflation in specific industries. Hence, those supply-oriented tax measures which aim to stimulate the growth of industrial capacity improve price performance and make lower unemployment possible. Conversely, measures which do not affect industrial capacity tend to have more limited price benefits.

[13]Richard A. Musgrave, *The Theory of Public Finance* (New York: McGraw-Hill, Inc., 1959), pp. 212-216.

The DRI model adheres to the philosophy of seeking to build models that represent the behavioral characteristics of the economy as fully as possible. As previous publications have indicated,[14] the macro models of the 1970s gradually incorporated several important new features that advancing understanding and a changing economic situation required. Earlier innovations, some of them based on the scientific work of the 1960s, included the use of a variable-coefficient input-output table as part of the model's simultaneous block to calculate industrial output and capacity utilization, an elaborate financial system representing the flows of funds of households and businesses, stage-of-processing pricing equations to carry particular cost increases more precisely into retail prices, a production-inventory-price loop, and an elaborate energy sector. The introduction of each of these innovations modified the basic behavioral characteristics of the model somewhat, with the aim of making the model reflect the current state of knowledge as found in the work not only of DRI, but of the academic and general research community. The model is meant to be as comprehensive a representation of the economic process as can be devised.

This approach is an alternative to pure "supply models." While models that are fully devoted to classical relationships among the factors of production may be appropriate for a very long-term analysis, understanding of inflation and the business cycle requires representation of demand, finance, stock flow adjustment processes, expectation formation, and other short-term elements. For analysis of the 1980s, whether for forecasting or policy purposes, purely supply-oriented models are inadequate. The current financial, energy, and business cycle situations are sufficiently far removed from equilibrium that the next decade will be heavily determined by the initial conditions and other short-run factors.

DRI's approach—to add carefully derived estimates of tax and other supply effects to an already elaborate representation of the economy—should provide as good estimates for the policy options as it is possible to obtain at this time. It should be recognized, however, that the new territory of supply economics, encompassing both the intermediate-term tax issues and the longer range questions of demography, saving, and private-public sector relations, is a very large one and will take years to fully explore. The extensions of the DRI model advanced here are only a few steps along the road to a full econometric representation of supply. "Supply multipliers" in the current model deal with only limited aspects and are not yet calculated over the decades over which they would ultimately be felt. Some of them are not yet as seasoned as the demand multipliers and it will take some years of

[14]See Otto Eckstein, "The DRI Model: Historical Perspective and an Overview," *The Great Recession* (Amsterdam: North-Holland Publishing Co., 1978), pp. 185-207.

scientific debate before agreement begins to emerge. At least the point has been reached where supply economics is, and should be, making itself felt in the "mainstream" models.

The supply equations in the DRI model can be classified under the following headings:

(1) The Supply of Labor;
(2) The Supply of Physical Capital;
(3) The Supply of Energy;
(4) The Supply of Materials; and
(5) The Supply of R&D.

In addition, supply is also determined by the effectiveness with which the factors of production are combined, giving rise to these additional equations:

(6) The Aggregate Production Function;
(7) The Determination of Industrial Capacities; and
(8) The Efficiency of Energy Use in Household and Business Purposes.

This list is far from exhaustive, of course. Numerous other equations are a part of the supply analysis, including the several hundred equations represented by the input-output, stage-of-processing, energy, and financial sectors. However, the list above includes the more significant equations in which the supply economics issues come into focus.

The relation of the supply issues to tax policy is summarized in Table 10.1. As research continues and supply multipliers settle toward a scientific consensus, the list may become more elaborate and the parameters may change.

3. The Supply of Labor

The DRI long-term forecasts employ a set of eight equations for the principal working-age population groups. The participation rates depend on time trends, cyclical conditions as measured by the unemployment rate, real wages, and for a few categories, the personal tax burden as represented by the average effective personal tax rate plus the employee share of payroll taxes and the average effective benefit levels of particular transfer programs such as AFDC and Social Security. These equations are used to forecast the long-term labor supply under normal conditions. These forecasts are preliminary to the macro model solutions.

The macro model contains one equation for labor supply which relies on the working-age population aged 18 to 64, the share of the population represented by males aged 25 to 54, the national unemployment rate, real wages, a time trend to reflect the sociological changes in the participation rate, and the

Table 10.1
Summary of Tax Effects on Supply in the DRI Model

Tax	Equations	Results of Statistical Testing	Description of Tax Effects on DRI Model
Corporate income tax rate	Investment, macro and industries, R&D	Well-established effect using Jorgenson theory	Affects rental price of capital and cash flow. Elasticity of investment with respect to revenue is -0.28 over the 1982-85 period.
Depreciation lives	Investment, R&D	Same	Same. Elasticity is -1.13.
Investment tax credit	Investment on equipment, R&D	Same	Same. Elasticity is -0.90.
Personal taxes	Labor supply	Significant at 5% level, using average effective rate of personal income and personal payroll taxes. Transfer payments affect supply of workers over 65 and of women aged 25 to 44. Period of fit affects parameter. Value in model is typical.	Elasticity of labor with respect to tax burden is -0.04. Elasticity of labor with respect to tax-induced change in real wages is -0.20.
	Potential output	Average affective burden of personal and payroll taxes is significant at significance level of 5%. Choice of period affects parameters, DRI model uses typical value obtained over various intervals and various specifications.	Elasticity of potential output with respect to personal tax rate is -.05. Extra potential raises productivity and lowers inflation.
	Savings deposits and bond holding of households	Savings flows affected by disposable income and by aftertax interest return.	Principally affects mortgage market and residential construction.
	Wages	Payroll tax burden has impact on compensation per hour.	Higher compensation affects prices and core inflation.

average effective personal and payroll tax rate (Table 10.2). This equation has simulation characteristics that are close to the properties of the eight-equation labor force model. It has an elasticity of supply with regard to real wages of 0.1, i.e., a 1% increase in real wages adds 0.1% to the number of workers, which at 1980 values would represent 100,000 individuals. The elasticity of the labor force with respect to the personal tax burden is -0.04, indicating that a 1% rise in the real tax burden discourages 0.04% of our workers from the labor force. Since 1965, the real tax burden has increased by almost 50%, driving 1.9 million people from the labor force according to the equation.

Table 10.2
Labor Force

Ordinary Least Squares

Quarterly (1956:1 to 1979:4)—96 Observations
Dependent Variable: DEPVARLC

	Coefficient	Standard error	T-Stat	Independent variable
	5.91041	0.1680	35.18	Constant
1)				PDL(QRULESSRUADJ(-1), 1,4,FAR)
/1.........	-0.0559273	0.005050		
/2.........	-0.0419455	0.003787		
/3.........	-0.0279637	0.002525		
/4.........	-0.0139818	0.001262		
Sum.......	-0.139818	0.01262	-11.08	
Average ...	1.00000	0.0	NC	
2)	0.00701561	0.0001457	48.16	PARTIPTREND
3)	3.81471	0.1246	30.62	log(NM25@54/N16&)
4)	0.287908	0.03770	7.637	log((JAHEADJEA(-1)/ PC(-1)))-log((TP+TWPER)/ TAXBASE)

R-Bar squared: 0.9761
Durbin-Watson statistic: 0.5961
Sum of squared residuals: 0.0588
Standard error of the regression: 0.02543 Normalized: 0.015

DEPVARLC =log(LHSLC/(0.70-LHSLC)), the participation rate, fitted in logit form,
LHSLC is the civilian labor force as a percentage of the civilian population age 16 and over,
QRULESSRUADJ is unemployment minus a demographic adjustment,
PARTIPTREND is the time trend used in the equation for the civilian labor force,
NM25@54 is the total male population aged 25 through 54 years,
N16& is the population aged 16 and over,
JAHEADJEA is the index of hourly earnings of private nonfarm production workers,
PC is the implicit price deflator for personal consumption expenditures,
TP is personal tax and nontax payments,
TWPER is personal contributions for social insurance,
TAXBASE is the personal income taxbase.

4. The Supply of Physical Capital

The supply of aggregate physical capital is determined by equations for producers' durable equipment (Table 10.3) and nonresidential construction. These equations follow the neoclassical Jorgenson theory which relies on a carefully calculated measure of the rental price of capital and on the level of expected output. The DRI model's investment equations have extended the Jorgenson approach by correcting the investment need for pollution abatement expenditures, by calculating the rental price of capital from the actual sources of corporate finance at any particular time as estimated from the flow of funds, by adding a debt service variable which indicates the existing burden of debt on corporate cash flow, and by introducing a surprise element into output which contrasts actual output with what was expected.

This equation shows a quite considerable effect of changes in the rental price of capital on the level of investment and therefore on the growth of the capital stock. For example, the mean elasticity of investment in plant and equipment with respect to the rental price of capital was found to be 0.8.

The same theoretical approach is used for the calculation of investment levels of 24 industries, including the two-digit manufacturing industries and such fields as utilities, communication, mining, and the various transportation industries. These equations serve both as a check on the macro estimates as well as inputs for the calculation of manufacturing capacity.

5. The Supply of Energy

The supply of energy is largely exogenous to the DRI macro model. Both the quantity and the price of oil from foreign sources must be considered largely exogenous, though there are some loops from activity levels of the industrial world to OPEC pricing. Domestic pricing is also largely exogenous because both oil and gas are still in the period of legislated decontrol price schedules. The supply of domestic energy is estimated endogenously in DRI's energy models, and these answers are entered into the macro analysis. The model does contain various simulation rules that represent the responses of energy prices and supply to changing macro conditions to permit fuller analysis of policies or other alternative scenarios, for to ignore such responses would attribute a stability to the economy that it does not possess. For example, the OPEC price responds proportionately to the domestic price level as represented by the GNP deflator. These simulation rules are not used in forecasting, where separate analyses determine these variables.

The model's energy sector serves three functions: to trace the effects of the exogenous energy prices to the retail stage, to provide a supply-demand check

Table 10.3
Investment (Producers' Durable Equipment)

Least Squares with First-Order Autocorrelation Correction
Quarterly (1958:1 to 1979:2)—86 Observations
Dependent Variable: IPDENR72

	Coefficient	Standard error	T-Stat	Independent variable
	-8.58286	2.701	-3.177	Constant
1)	-0.0323568	0.03990	-0.8109	KNPDENR72(-1)
2)	0.128474	0.02804	4.582	KNPDENR72(-1)*UCAPFRBM
3)				PDLR(DEBTSERVICE(-1),1,7,FAR)
/1.........	-5.51410	4.432		
/2.........	-4.72637	3.799		
/3.........	-3.93864	3.166		
/4.........	-3.15091	2.532		
/5.........	-2.36319	1.899		
/6.........	-1.57546	1.266		
/7.........	-0.787728	0.6331		
Sum.......	-22.0564	17.73	-1.244	
Average ...	2.00000	0.0	NC	
4)	-0.0486685	0.02073	-2.347	QSTAR-LETOUTPUTPABE
5)				PDL(LETIPDENR72PQC(-3),2,6, FAR)
/3.........	0.000424575	0.001225		
/4.........	0.00233408	0.0006041		
/5.........	0.00345148	0.0005461		
/6.........	0.00377677	0.0006523		
/7.........	0.00330996	0.0006341		
/8.........	0.00205103	0.0004223		
Sum.......	0.0153479	0.002534	6.057	
Average ...	2.87090	0.4903	5.855	
	0.797527	0.07308	10.91	RHO

R-Bar squared: 0.9963
F-statistic (7,78): 3254
Durbin-Watson statistic: 1.8293
Sum of squared residuals: 118.4
Standard error of the regression: 1.232 Normalized: 0.01940

IPDENR72 is nonresidential investment in producers' durable equipment in 1972 dollars,
KNPDENR72 is the real net capital stock of producers' durable equipment in 1972 dollars,
UCAPFRBM is total manufacturing capacity utilization,
DEBTSERVICE is interest cost on outstanding debt,
QSTAR is the expectations variable for real output,
LETOUTPUTPABE is real output factored up by the PABE (pollution abatement expenditures by U.S. business on capital account) ratio,
LETIPDENR72PQC is the flexible accelerator term for IPDENR72,
RHO is the first-order autocorrelation correction parameter.

to see if available supplies can sustain particular levels of economic activity, and to determine the effects on potential GNP and productivity. The price effects are estimated by a series of equations which link the production and import prices of coal, natural gas, and oil through input-output coefficients to industrial wholesale and the pertinent consumer prices. The changed prices impact real activity and the system as a whole, partly depending on the monetary policy response.

To test for the adequacy of energy supplies, the model calculates and cumulates the demand for energy by principal sources, including oil, gas, coal, and electricity. The total energy requirement is compared to the energy supply to test for particular model solutions. If supply falls short of demand and if prices are still controlled, an energy shortage develops which must be allocated to particular tailormade solutions. Consistency can be achieved by pulling down aggregate activity, by imposing allocations or rationing in specific markets, or by letting delivery conditions deteriorate and thereby creating some indirect inflation. The effect on potential GNP is measured by energy's role in the production function. As higher prices lead to energy conservation, there is less energy input into the economy and therefore less output. Because the Cobb-Douglas function does not contain interaction terms, the effect may be understated.

6. The Supply of Materials

Because the DRI model takes the market approach, prices are the principal vehicle for supply conditions to affect the economy. A scarce supply of materials, such as steel, chemicals, oil, lumber, etc., is shown through high utilization rates, which increase finished goods prices through the stage-of-processing price equations. Besides the utilization effects, the model also contains a separate channel for vendor performance, the well-known measure of delivery conditions in industrial markets. Poor vendor performance acts in the model to raise industrial prices and to stimulate inventory hoarding.

In considering the determination of the supply of materials, processed materials must be distinguished from raw materials. The supply of processed materials is determined by the growth in capital stocks and by technology. An industry's capital stock is determined from equations explaining the level of investment. The supply of raw materials is modeled through prices: agricultural commodities and world oil are reflected in exogenous price variables; other raw materials prices are endogenous, moved by the strength of demand, and on the supply side by strike variables. DRI's micro models of industrial and agricultural commodities do model the availability and costs of supply very elaborately, and this work is an input to the materials price forecasts in the macro model.

7. The Supply of R&D

The DRI model incorporates the stock of technical knowledge, as measured by the cumulated research and development outlays of governments and private industry, as one of the inputs in the aggregate production function. Thus, thc volume of R&D investment affects the growth of potential GNP. The stock of R&D, which is treated analogously to the stock of physical capital, is assumed to depreciate over 10 years. In a competitive world, a society which does not advance its technology will lose its relative industrial position, and therefore its growth of potential will diminish. Thus, the stock of knowledge must be treated as a depreciating asset. Technology is also required to offset the decline in exhaustible resources. Investment in R&D is determined analogously to other investment decisions, using an equation embodying the Jorgenson approach.

8. The Aggregate Production Function: Potential GNP

Potential GNP, the supply measure of the economy's ability to produce goods and services, is estimated by an aggregate production function. The factors treated explicitly are capital, labor, energy, and the stock of research and development capital. Research and development is partly capital enhancing and partly labor enhancing. To reflect the influence of embodied technology further, the average age of the capital stock helps determine potential output. The cyclical influence on factor use is measured by the utilization rate of manufacturing capacity and by the change in average hours worked. The deleterious effect of the tax system on productivity is measured by the average effective rate of personal and payroll taxes.

Potential GNP is estimated in a two-step procedure which facilitates the introduction of the supply of energy and of the stock of research and development into the aggregate production function framework. Step 1 established a Cobb-Douglas production function which includes the four inputs—capital, labor, energy, and R&D. The average age of capital is introduced as an adjustment to the capital stock. The use of the capital stock in any period is determined by the utilization rate of manufacturing capacity. This equation is fitted in the form of the output-to-labor ratio in order to overcome the problems of multicollinearity (Table 10.4).

The coefficients derived from this Cobb-Douglas function are used to calculate an index of composite factor inputs which is then employed in a second equation shown in Table 10.5. This equation explains the "residual," the measure of change in the productivity of all factor inputs. This equation

Table 10.4
Potential GNP: Step 1

Ordinary Least Squares
Quarterly (1957:1 to 1979:1)—89 Observations
Dependent Variable: NEWLHSGNP72A

	Coefficient	Standard error	T-Stat	Independent variable
	1.39819	0.01486	94.12	Constant
1)	0.00151723	6.283E-05	24.15	TIME
2)	0.0481635	0.01035	4.652	log(DTFUELSALLB/ EHHHOURSA)
3)	0.290869	0.005939	48.98	log(UCAPFRBM*KADJ(-1)/ EHHHOURSA)

R-Bar squared: 0.9874
Durbin-Watson statistic: 0.4923
Sum of squared residuals: 0.0087
Standard error of the regression: 0.01012 Normalized: 0.005

NEWLHSGNP72A =log(GNP72/EHHHOURSA)-0.08*log(TOTALR&DSTOCK72(-1)/ EHHHOURSA),
GNP72 is gross national product in 1972 dollars,
TOTALR&DSTOCK72 is total stock of research and development,
TIME is the time trend, 1947:1 = 1.0,
DTFUELSALLB is the demand for all fuels, total, all sectors,
EHHHOURSA is total worker hours,
UCAPFRBM is total manufacturing capacity utilization,
KADJ is the age-adjusted capital stock.

uses time trends to carry the effects of disembodied technology, with separate trends to reflect the breaks of productivity which occurred in 1967 and 1973. In addition, the equation contains a measure of the personal tax burden to reflect the tax effect on the efficiency of resource utilization as measured by total factor productivity.

The aggregate production function contains an implicit estimate for high-employment labor productivity. To estimate actual productivity, it is necessary to estimate its short-run variation around this potential trend (Table 10.6). The equation uses the utilization rate of manufacturing capacity and the "surprise" component in expectations about real GNP to explain the cyclical swings. Short-run productivity is also adversely affected by increases in the price of energy.

To measure potential output, the cyclical variables are set at their full employment values, which for this purpose are defined to be a manufacturing workweek of 40-3/4 hours, a full-employment unemployment rate following the Council of Economic Advisers' definition, and a utilization rate of manufacturing capacity of 87%. The resultant series is still too volatile and therefore is smoothed by a second-order Pascal lag with a decay factor of 0.7.

Table 10.5
Potential GNP: Step 2

Ordinary Least Squares

Quarterly (1957:1 to 1979:1)—89 Observations
Dependent Variable: LHSGNP72[1]

	Coefficient	Standard error	T-Stat	Independent variable
	1.28416	0.04866	26.39	Constant
1)	0.00189295	0.0001432	13.21	TIME
2)	0.336940	0.1432	2.353	log(HPM/HPM(-1))
3)	-0.000370151	0.0002303	-1.607	TIMEONE
4)	0.00918571	0.005368	1.711	TIMETWO
5)	-0.0518671	0.02302	-2.253	log((TP+TWPER)/TAXBASE)

R-Bar squared: 0.9497
F-statistic (5,83): 333.6
Durbin-Watson statistic: 0.7874
Sum of squared residuals: 0.006812
Standard error of the regression: 0.009059 Normalized: 0.005921

LHSGNP72 =log(GNP72/EHHHOURS)-0.08*log(TOTALR&DSTOCK72(-1)/EHHHOURS)-0.05*log(DTFUELSALLB/EHHHOURS)-0.29*log(UCAPFRBM*KADJ(-1)/EHHHOURS),
GNP72 is gross national product in 1972 dollars,
EHHHOURS is total worker hours,
TOTALR&DSTOCK72 is total stock of research and development,
DTFUELSALLB is demand for all fuels, total, all sectors,
UCAPFRBM is total manufacturing capacity utilization,
KADJ is age-adjusted capital stock,
TIME is the time trend, 1947:1 = 1.0,
HPM is weekly hours of manufacturing production workers,
TIMEONE is a time trend for potential GNP,
TIMETWO is a time trend for potential GNP,
TP is personal tax and nontax payments,
TWPER is personal contributions for social insurance,
TAXBASE is the personal income taxbase.

9. Industrial Capacity and Other Supply Effects

Shortages of industrial capacity in materials industries proved to be an effective supply constraint in 1971-73 and 1978-79. The DRI model estimates the capacities of manufacturing, materials, primary processing, and advanced processing industries from the investment estimates of the pertinent two-digit manufacturing industries. Through the embedded input-output table, the model calculates production for these sectors of manufacturing, which are then combined with the capacity estimates to calculate the utilization rates.

The impact of utilization rates on the economy is felt through several channels: first, they are the demand variables in several of the price equations in the stage-of-processing sector of the model. Second, utilization rates are

Table 10.6
Productivity

Least Squares with First-Order Autocorrelation Correction

Quarterly (1962:1 to 1979:1)—69 Observations
Dependent Variable: LHSJQ%MHNF[1]

	Coefficient	Standard error	T-Stat	Independent variable
	-2.10402	0.04946	-42.54	Constant
1)	0.00150552	0.0001594	9.442	TIME
2)	0.00800536	0.003455	2.317	1/(1.1-UCAPFRBM)
3)	-0.0349436	0.02103	-1.662	log((TP+TWPER)/TAXBASE)
4)	-0.432759	0.1056	-4.097	log(QSTAR/LETOUTPUTPABE)
5)	-0.0614098	0.01932	-3.178	log((WPI05(-1)/PC&I&G(-1))/ (WPI05(-5)/PC&I&G(-5)))
	0.716376	0.09638	7.432	RHO

R-Bar squared: 0.9540
F-statistic (6,62): 236.0
Durbin-Watson statistic: 2.3156
Sum of squared residuals: 0.001940
Standard error of the regression: 0.005594 Normalized: 0.003043

LHSJQ%MHNF =log(JQ%MHNF)-log(GNP72FE/(52.0*0.001*HPMFE*((1.0-.01*RUFE)*LC))),
JQ%MHNF is the index of output per hour of all persons in the nonfarm business sector,
GNP72FE is the full-employment level of real gross national product,
HPMFE is weekly hours of manufacturing production workers—full employment,
RUFE is the unemployment rate at full employment,
LC is the civilian labor force,
TIME is the time trend, 1947:1 = 1.0,
UCAPFRBM is total manufacturing capacity utilization,
TP is personal tax and nontax payments,
TWPER is personal contributions for social insurance,
TAXBASE is the personal income taxbase,
QSTAR is the expectations variable for real output,
LETOUTPUTPABE is real output factored up by the PABE (pollution abatement expenditures by U.S. business on capital account) ratio,
WPI05 is the wholesale price index for fuels and related products and power,
PC&I&G is the implicit price deflator excluding the foreign trade sector,
RHO is the first-order autocorrelation correction parameter.

important determinants of vendor performance, a measure of delivery conditions in industrial markets. Vendor performance, in turn, has important effects on industrial prices as well as on inventory policies which, in turn, strongly affect the demand for industrial output. Thus, there is a significant sub-loop in the model from industrial capacity to prices to inventories and back to prices. Finally, utilization affects profitability and productivity, and thereby affects the economy as a whole.

Among other supply-oriented features of the DRI model, the supply of finance should be singled out. The behavior of the mortgage market, which itself is mainly moved by the supply of personal saving and the partly policy-determined structure of interest rates, strongly affects the housing industry. Nonresidential fixed investment is also affected by the supply of finance, mainly through disequilibria in the balance sheets of the corporate sector. Consumption of durable goods is affected by real interest rates and the balancc sheet position of households.

CHAPTER 11

WILL CORE INFLATION COME DOWN?

For 15 years, the core inflation rate has deteriorated. Is there a realistic prospect that this trend can be reversed, productivity will pick up, OPEC become more moderate, inflation expectations abate, government policies stop adding to costs and prices? Certainly the society has an improved understanding of its problems and politicians are saying the right things. But will the nation really move to a better course? An assessment of the more factual side of the prospects and policy needs should prove useful.

1. The Demand Issues

The review of the historical record showed that excessively stimulative budgets and increases of the money supply contributed importantly to the development of core inflation. Noninflationary budget and monetary policies are essential ingredients of any program to bring down core inflation.

Demand management can be defined in terms of its target unemployment rate. Unemployment is still the most comprehensive measure of total resource utilization in the economy and is a good gauge of the relative balance of aggregate demand and supply for the economy as a whole. While disparities between the growth of labor and physical capital can create an extra pressure on the price level, it is not unreasonable to assume that future capital growth will cure this imbalance or that imports of industrial materials will neutralize it.

1. "Full-Employment" and "Natural" Unemployment Rates

The "full-employment" unemployment rate is the rate which describes normal unemployment allowing for functional turnover and search periods. It changes with the population structure by age, sex, and work experience.

Before the big influx of new workers to the labor force, the "full-employment" rate was approximately 4½%. It has risen substantially since then and is somewhat over 5% at this time. The 1980s will see improvement in this rate as workers, on average, become more experienced now that the big influx of young workers is behind us, but women will continue to stream into the labor force.

To avoid demand inflation, however, the labor market must be kept considerably more slack than the "full-employment" rate would indicate. The "natural" unemployment in Friedman's formulation was defined as that ratc which will leave the inflation rate unchanged at its expected value.[1]

The appearance of shocks requires that demand and shock effects be separated. For the present analysis, the natural unemployment rate is the description of the state of aggregate demand which avoids any contribution, positive or negative, of demand on actual inflation, and therefore ultimately on core inflation.

This natural rate of unemployment is defined formally by equation (19) in Chapter 2. It can be estimated empirically from equation (27) of Chapter 3. By solving that demand equation so the left-hand side equals zero and assuming a utilization rate of industrial capacity in the normal range of 80 to 85%, an estimate for the natural unemployment rate of 7.2% is obtained. The full-employment rate is 5.1%, but an additional 2.1% of unemployment is needed to offset the inflationary bias of the economic system.[2] This bias has many sources. Wages rise beyond the productivity trend even when unemployment exceeds the full-employment rate. Prices in the more oligopolistic industries respond fully to cost increases even if there is excess capacity. Government reduces the degree of competition through numerous forms of protectionism. And the income benefits programs such as unemployment insurance, public assistance, and Social Security provide workers an incentive to become unemployed and to remain in that status for extended periods.

Compared to the historical goals, an unemployment rate near 7% is a very disappointing objective. It is also substantially higher than the levels that the political process is likely to find acceptable. Consequently, a program to bring down core inflation must include measures that improve the economy's structure. These include policies to bring down frictional and search unemployment of such special groups as young workers, as well as policies to

[1]Milton Friedman, "The Role of Monetary Policy," *American Economic Review,* March 1968, pp. 1-17.

[2]The detailed specification of the demand equation (27) can be varied by altering the lag distributions, suppressing the utilization variable or replacing it with an alternative measure of non-labor resource utilization, or switching the particular measure of unemployment. Such changes produce equations which imply slightly different natural rates of unemployment. The range of values found in equations of comparable statistical quality is from 6.8 to 7.4%, with most clustered somewhat above 7%.

reduce the inflation created by monopoly elements, reductions of government protectionism, and changes in income benefit programs to reduce their incentives for workers to be unemployed.

2. *The Noninflationary Unemployment Rate*

If a 7% natural unemployment rate is a discouraging target, it is noninflationary only if there are no shocks to provide other inflation impulses. But shocks have certainly been the pattern of the day and if no other solutions are found, a further increment of unemployment will be necessary to neutralize the inflationary effects of shocks.

Equation (27) can be solved to calculate the unemployment rate necessary to create a deflationary impact on the price level sufficient to offset shocks of varying severity. The solution implies an increase in unemployment of 0.4 percentage points to neutralize a shock of 1% a year. This would bring the noninflationary unemployment rate to 7.6%. Should the shock factors total 1.5% a year, unemployment would have to be 7.9%, while a shock rate of 2% a year would require an increment of unemployment of 1.0% over the natural rate, for a total of 8.2%. A reasonable expectation for the shocks of the 1980s is an average annual value of 1½%, implying a noninflationary unemployment rate of 7.9%.

3. *Prospects for Demand Management*

The analysis shows that the noninflationary unemployment goals under conditions of shock inflation are so high that they are politically impossible. The country is hardly likely to stand still for demand management which seeks to hold the unemployment rate above 7½%. Consequently, there must be a search for other approaches to lowering core inflation, presumably on the supply side. If the attempt were made, the economic condition of disadvantaged groups would be so poor that new programs would be instituted that would worsen the natural rate of unemployment further.

But will demand management be able to make its necessary contribution to the disinflation process? Can unemployment be held in the neighborhood of 7%, where supply policies can still work to bring down core inflation?

The present approach to monetary policy is consistent with this kind of conservative approach. The most recent monetary targets, designed to apply to the year 1980, called for a growth in the narrow money supply, M1B, in the range of 4 to 6½%, and the Federal Reserve hopes to bring down even this modest rate in the years ahead at a rate of half a point a year or so. While the velocity of the money supply is both unstable and increasing under the stimulus of technological and regulatory changes, the money targets, even at their upper limit, will be consistent with a growth in nominal GNP of no more than 8 to 10%. Given the Federal Reserve's current determination and the near-term prospects of a core inflation rate of 9%, monetary policy will keep the real level of interest rates sufficiently high to hold the economy slack and to keep unemployment in noninflatonary territory.

The prospects for fiscal policy are rather more uncertain. There is a strong desire for large tax reductions of all sorts, both designed to stimulate supply and to give general relief from current burdens. Military spending is rising rapidly, and there is the wish to bring civilian spending under better control. President Reagan has raised the tough issues, but it will take several years to see if his program is carried out. The best available measure of fiscal impact remains the "full-employment budget," a description of the budget that would prevail if there were full employment. But to calculate its noninflationary values, one must calculate it using the noninflationary unemployment rate. Assuming that figure to fall in the 7.2-to-8.2% range, there is only a small prospect that the budget will be in balance in the years ahead at noninflationary levels of unemployment. Thus, monetary policy is likely to be working to overcome continuing modest doses of budget stimulus. While the extraordinary restraint exercised in the 1980 recession in avoiding significant measures of countercyclical stimulus is ample evidence that "fine-tuning" for full employment is gone, it would be sanguine to assume that fully noninflationary demand policies lie ahead.

4. More Instability?

The combination of mildly stimulating fiscal policy with a gradual reduction in the growth of the money supply may achieve an appropriate average level of demand, but probably with a highly unstable pattern. The demand for money will have a tendency to grow faster than the policy targets, with short-term variations in money growth around the trend created by minor variations in consumer and business spending, small price shocks, impulses originating abroad, and data ambiguities created by inevitably inaccurate seasonal adjustment at such times as tax payment dates. The Federal Reserve will be able to adjust bank reserve growth gently for many of these variations. But it is highly likely that the correction will have to be more brutal every few years, as the rhythm of the business cycle collides with the desire for stable money growth, and prices surge due to unstable energy or food supplies.

Unfortunately, instability of output reduces the growth of aggregate supply because it hurts investment. Capital becomes costly and scarce in the credit crunches, and the basis for long-term investment plans is undercut by recessions. Reduced investment diminishes potential output and productivity, and thereby worsens core inflation.

The challenge to demand management is very great in the 1980s. Unemployment must be kept relatively high until the economy's structure is improved and core inflation is moving down substantially. Yet this moderate level of demand must be achieved without the productivity-disrupting credit crunches and recessions. Only if budget policy achieves a better fiscal performance will the Federal Reserve be able to achieve the orderly reduction in money growth which is indeed central to a successful program to lower core inflation.

2. The Shock Issues

The historical review revealed that shocks played a major role in creating core inflation, and indeed were the dominant influence in the last decade. Will the shocks be smaller in the 1980s or perhaps even approach the happy condition of zero that prevailed in prior decades?

The energy prospects remain negative but should be less extreme than in the years since the ascendancy of OPEC. World oil prices cannot keep increasing at the rates that have been typical since 1973, or if they do, they will induce sufficient conservation and substitution to cut oil imports to small magnitudes. Thus, an improvement of energy shocks is a realistic projection, but an end to energy shocks would be wildly optimistic.

The "self-inflicted wounds," in Arthur Okun's vivid phrase, of government policies that directly boost costs are also widely understood today, and there is a strong determination in the political process if not to end them, at least to hold them to a minimum. Large increases in Social Security taxes are recognized to be inflationary, and the Congress is searching for ways both to find new tax resources and to bring some limits to benefit increases. Thus, the probable path of Social Security tax rates is more favorable in the 1980s than it was in the last decade. The minimum wage is barely keeping pace with other wages, and its damage to youth employment is also generally understood; thus, this particular shock is likely to remain insignificant. Other forms of government-imposed cost increases, which are not modeled quantitatively in the core inflation analysis, are also likely to be more favorable in the years ahead. The peak has clearly passed in the country's enthusiasm for expanding the scope of government regulation, though a major retreat is unlikely and the best that can be hoped for is a more sensitive administration of the enormous reservoir of potential regulatory powers now on the statute books.

The decline of the dollar in foreign exchange markets has also been a source of inflationary shocks, though the total effect has been quite minor. Whether it will be a continuing source of inflation will depend on our success in bringing down the core inflation rate. If it is not improved, the dollar will gradually sink against the currencies of countries with lower core rates, particularly Japan and West Germany. The U.S. international trade position will also suffer, and we will be losing the benefit to productivity performance which can only come from a competitive edge in world markets.

3. The Prospect for Labor Costs

The future trend of labor costs will be partly determined by the degree of recovery in the economy's productivity performance. Wages have lagged behind prices for the last three years, even if prices are measured by the deflator of consumer expenditures rather than the biased consumer price index. With a new business cycle upswing underway in the early 80's, and with price expectations matching or exceeding the recent increase of wages, a realistic projection must call for a modest wage acceleration. In the absence of yet another and more prolonged recession or the imposition of wage-price controls, the realistic prospect for wage increases for the first half of the 1980s is in the 10% range. These are somewhat larger figures than the experience of the second half of the 1970s, and taken alone, point toward worsening core inflation.

The prospect for productivity is uncertain, but is at least somewhat subject to our own decisions. The reasons for the loss of productivity performance are generally understood, though there is much controversy about the relative importance of the various factors.[3] They include the stagnation in the capital labor ratio, demographic changes, direct and indirect effects attributable to the surge of energy costs, a diminution of investment in R&D, and the extraordinary instability of the last dozen years. The policies discussed in Chapters 7 and 8 would restore a more normal historical growth in the capital-labor ratio, allowing each worker to be equipped with increasing amounts of machinery and technology as they were throughout our long history of economic progress. The demographic factor is also somewhat more favorable because of the maturing labor force, and probably the worst damage of the energy revolution is behind us. Thus, it is not unreasonable to project that the

[3]Edward F. Denison, *Accounting for Slower Economic Growth* (Washington: Brookings Institution, 1979); J.R. Norsworthy, Michael J. Harper, and Kent Kunze, "The Slowdown in Productivity Growth," Brookings Economic Papers, 1979:2, pp. 387-421; and Robin Siegel, "Why Has Productivity Slowed Down?" *Data Resources Review,* March 1979, pp. 59-65.

productivity trend will stage a significant comeback and be as much as a point or so better than it was in recent years.

Combining a small acceleration in the wage trend with modest improvement in the productivity trend yields a path for unit labor costs which is about the same or a little changed from the recent history. This is not an area which yields much optimism on the country's prospects for an improving core inflation rate during the first half of the decade. In the later years, the pattern of unit labor costs will, of course, be determined by the intervening history. If core inflation can be brought down early, wage increases will be smaller in the later 1980s, and productivity performance will offset a larger share of them. But policies will have to be strong and effective in the next five years in order to reach that outcome.

4. *The Prospect for Capital Costs*

The trend in capital costs is determined by the historical inflation rate because interest rates are largely determined by price expectations, and these expectations are largely formed from observed reality. If other dimensions of the inflation problem are dealt with successfully, price expectations will improve and interest rates will reflect this change. On the other hand, since the preceding discussion raises no more than glimmers of hope about demand management, shocks, and labor costs, there is little basis for optimism about future interest rates.

Policy does have the ability to reduce the capital cost element of core inflation directly. The tax reforms discussed in Chapters 7 and 8 would lower the rental price of capital, and this lower capital cost would gradually aid actual prices, boost investment and productivity, and thereby also help unit labor costs. The maximum benefit that can be achieved from this approach is limited, an improvement of 2% for the decade in the maximum policies discussed in Chapter 8, an improvement of 1% a year in the more moderate and politically feasible policies of Chapter 7. This is hardly enough to offset the probable average shock values and therefore leaves the analysis with the pessimistic conclusion that it will indeed be very difficult to achieve a significant reduction in core inflation.

5. *Could We Do Better? Some Open Issues*

The thrust of the current analysis is two-fold: first, the assessment for inflation improvement is, on the whole, quite pessimistic. Second, supply measures are absolutely essential to complement cautious demand management to achieve any lowering of the core inflation rate.

Could the analysis be wrong? Could the theory of the economy's behavior, both in concept and empirical representation, be too gloomy and overlook some more cheerful possibilities? Are there policy approaches not considered here that might achieve dramatic results? After all, economic science was not particularly successful in anticipating the continuing deterioration of inflation; could it be equally unsuccessful in anticipating a coming improvement?

There are several places where the analysis of this book could ultimately prove to be too pessimistic. First, and most controversial, is the question of expectations. The rational expectations school argues that a change in economic policy regime will alter the process by which workers and investors form their price expectations. Even if the empirical evidence cited in Chapter 9 is persuasive about the slow learning processes revealed by the historical record, this school of thought would argue that the future will be different. Until the experiment is actually run, a firm conclusion cannot be asserted, and so an opening for hope remains that expectations can be improved more dramatically than the historical formulas would imply.

The rate of wage increase is another area where results could be less inflationary than the material presented in this book. As discussed in Chapter 9, the wage record since the OPEC revolution shows surprisingly modest results, including large declines in real wages. While the causes for this wage slowdown cannot be determined precisely, those same causes may continue to work in the future, creating continuing declines in real wages. If productivity performance can be partially restored, such extraordinary wage behavior would bring down core inflation, albeit at a considerable social cost in falling living standards.

A third area of uncertainty is in the conversion of the cost trends embodied in the core rate into actual inflation performance. Industrial markets may become more competitive in the years ahead under the pressure of foreign competition and more conservative monetary and fiscal policies. Businesses may not find it possible to pass forward all of the core increases into higher prices, thereby introducing another loop for decelerating the wage-price spiral and permitting an improvement in expectations. In particular, there is only very limited empirical evidence on the relation between rising capital costs and prices. If the pull of demand is weak, firms may not be able to incorporate high interest rates and rising plant and equipment prices in the prices they charge their customers. It is only if there is a continuing need for expansion of capacity that economic theory argues that capital costs will be fully passed on in output prices.

Other developments could also be favorable, of course. We may be fortunate, through technological or political developments, in overcoming the cost pressures coming from energy. The surprising slowdown in productivity may be followed by an equally surprising acceleration. But there is little present sign of any of these hopes materializing.

6. New Types of Policies?

If the challenge to demand management is too great and the possibilities of supply policies too limited for quick results, can other approaches be found? The gloomy prospect sketched here invites the creative search for new solutions.

Tax-based incomes policies (TIPS) pose enormous, perhaps insuperable, administrative obstacles, mainly because the information-keeping system of business does not produce the data that would allow a firm's federal tax liability to be based on the firm's actual wage and price conduct with reasonable precision. But if there are no other plausible solutions, even a sloppy TIPS policy may be worth a try despite the damage it may do to the solidity of the tax system.

Comprehensive, mandatory, strongly enforced wage-price controls, applied for a sufficient time period, would change the rules of the game and might dramatically change expectations to break the back of core inflation. But experience suggests that the cost of controls is very high, and that the political process is unable to sustain a meaningful wage-price program for more than a few months. Yet to be effective, the minimum period of controls would have to be greater than three years, so that a full wage and price cycle has had time to run its course.

Large-scale, supply-side personal tax reductions have also been advanced as possible solutions to the inflation problem. If labor supply were to increase dramatically and work effort to become more productive through reduction of marginal tax rates, the core inflation rate would be brought down. So far, however, the empirical evidence shows only small responses of labor supply and productivity to personal tax changes, far too small to decisively affect the core inflation rate, and difficult to finance through spending reductions of sufficient magnitude to avoid the inflationary effects created by the net increase of demand. Stimuli to personal saving and reductions in the taxation of capital gains are also currently receiving a serious hearing. While they would produce effects in the right direction by encouraging the availability of investible capital, the benefits would probably be on a small scale in relation to the core inflation problem.

What is the most positive statement that can reasonably be advanced to summarize our prospects? I believe it is this: nothing is fully predictable in human affairs and nothing is inevitable in an economy's development. Better luck could combine with carefully designed efforts to augment the economy's ability to produce and with cautious demand policies to bring down the core inflation rate. If we can reverse its deterioration and begin the path to improvement in the next few years, we will have ample reason for pride.

Historical Data

NEWVARIABLES	60:1	60:2	60:3	60:4	61:1	61:2	61:3	61:4	62:1	62:2	62:3	62:4	63:1	63:2	63:3	63:4
CORE	3.3	3.1	3.0	2.8	2.5	2.3	2.0	1.8	1.5	1.4	1.3	1.2	1.2	1.2	1.1	1.1
SHOCK	-0.2	-0.0	0.2	0.4	0.4	0.1	-0.1	-0.2	-0.1	0.2	0.2	0.1	0.1	0.0	-0.1	-0.3
DEMAND	-1.7	-1.3	-1.8	-1.7	-1.4	-1.5	-0.7	-0.8	-0.6	-0.3	-0.3	0.0	-0.0	-0.2	0.4	0.5
RCPIUYAMACRO	1.4	1.8	1.4	1.4	1.5	0.9	1.2	0.7	0.9	1.3	1.2	1.3	1.2	1.0	1.4	1.4
JAHEADJEAFE	0.74	0.75	0.76	0.76	0.77	0.78	0.79	0.80	0.81	0.81	0.82	0.83	0.84	0.85	0.86	0.86
JQ%MHNFFE79	0.78	0.78	0.78	0.78	0.79	0.79	0.79	0.80	0.80	0.80	0.81	0.81	0.82	0.82	0.83	0.83
IFIXNRCOSTEXP85	1.9	1.8	1.8	1.6	1.2	0.7	0.2	0.0	-0.1	-0.1	-0.1	-0.1	-0.1	-0.0	0.0	0.1
GNP72FERAW	761.9	772.8	778.3	784.9	790.7	796.4	799.6	804.0	809.2	814.2	821.6	827.5	835.1	842.3	850.0	857.9
GNP72FE	759.9	766.2	772.6	779.2	785.8	792.4	798.7	804.8	810.6	816.3	822.3	828.4	834.6	840.9	847.4	854.2
	64:1	64:2	64:3	64:4	65:1	65:2	65:3	65:4	66:1	66:2	66:3	66:4	67:1	67:2	67:3	67:4
CORE	1.1	1.0	0.9	0.8	0.7	0.6	0.6	0.6	0.7	0.9	1.0	1.2	1.4	1.5	1.6	1.6
SHOCK	-0.1	-0.2	-0.2	-0.2	-0.1	0.2	0.4	0.5	0.9	0.7	0.7	0.4	0.1	0.1	-0.1	-0.1
DEMAND	0.5	0.7	0.4	0.6	0.6	0.8	0.8	0.7	0.8	1.1	1.5	2.0	1.5	0.9	1.2	1.3
RCPIUYAMACRO	1.5	1.5	1.1	1.2	1.2	1.6	1.8	1.8	2.4	2.7	3.2	3.6	2.9	2.6	2.7	2.9
JAHEADJEAFE	0.87	0.88	0.89	0.90	0.91	0.92	0.93	0.93	0.94	0.95	0.96	0.97	0.98	0.99	1.01	1.02
JQ%MHNFFE79	0.84	0.84	0.85	0.86	0.86	0.87	0.87	0.88	0.89	0.89	0.90	0.91	0.92	0.92	0.93	0.94
IFIXNRCOSTEXP85	0.1	0.1	0.1	0.0	-0.0	-0.0	0.0	0.1	0.4	0.8	1.1	1.5	1.9	2.1	2.2	2.1
GNP72FERAW	866.9	880.8	886.5	894.3	902.0	915.1	927.5	938.6	945.3	956.9	969.3	981.3	989.0	1000.7	1011.8	1024.5
GNP72FE	861.3	869.2	877.4	885.6	893.9	902.7	912.0	921.9	931.7	941.7	952.1	962.8	973.4	984.1	995.0	1006.1
	68:1	68:2	68:3	68:4	69:1	69:2	69:3	69:4	70:1	70:2	70:3	70:4	71:1	71:2	71:3	71:4
CORE	1.6	1.8	2.0	2.2	2.5	2.8	3.1	3.5	3.8	4.1	4.3	4.3	4.4	4.3	4.3	4.2
SHOCK	0.0	0.1	0.2	0.4	0.4	0.5	0.5	0.5	0.6	0.3	0.4	0.3	0.6	0.8	0.7	0.6
DEMAND	2.0	2.2	2.2	2.1	1.9	2.2	1.9	1.7	1.9	1.6	1.1	1.0	-0.2	-0.7	-0.7	-1.3
RCPIUYAMACRO	3.6	4.1	4.4	4.7	4.8	5.5	5.6	5.7	6.2	6.0	5.7	5.6	4.8	4.4	4.3	3.5
JAHEADJEAFE	1.03	1.04	1.05	1.07	1.08	1.09	1.11	1.12	1.14	1.15	1.17	1.19	1.20	1.22	1.24	1.26
JQ%MHNFFE79	0.94	0.95	0.96	0.96	0.97	0.97	0.98	0.98	0.99	1.00	1.00	1.01	1.01	1.02	1.02	1.03
IFIXNRCOSTEXP85	2.0	2.1	2.2	2.6	2.9	3.3	3.9	4.5	5.0	5.5	5.8	5.9	5.9	5.7	5.3	5.0
GNP72FERAW	1030.1	1041.4	1046.7	1055.6	1065.7	1075.7	1091.2	1102.2	1114.0	1121.5	1133.5	1140.8	1147.8	1154.0	1162.2	1169.9
GNP72FE	1016.8	1027.5	1037.7	1047.5	1057.2	1066.9	1077.2	1087.9	1098.9	1109.7	1120.6	1131.3	1141.5	1151.2	1160.5	1169.4

	72:1	72:2	72:3	72:4	73:1	73:2	73:3	73:4	74:1	74:2	74:3	74:4	75:1	75:2	75:3	75:4
CORE	4.2	4.2	4.2	4.1	4.1	4.2	4.4	4.7	5.1	5.6	6.3	7.0	7.6	8.0	8.0	8.0
SHOCK...............	0.6	0.7	1.0	1.1	2.0	2.8	3.3	3.6	4.0	4.0	3.6	3.6	1.7	1.2	0.9	0.8
DEMAND	-1.3	-1.6	-2.0	-1.8	-2.1	-1.4	-1.0	0.1	0.8	0.9	1.6	1.6	1.7	0.5	-0.2	-1.4
RCPIUYAMACRO	3.5	3.2	3.1	3.4	4.1	5.6	6.8	8.3	9.9	10.5	11.5	12.2	11.1	9.7	8.7	7.3
JAHEADJEAFE.......	1.28	1.29	1.31	1.33	1.35	1.37	1.39	1.41	1.43	1.46	1.49	1.52	1.55	1.58	1.61	1.65
JQ%MHNFFE79.......	1.03	1.03	1.04	1.04	1.05	1.05	1.05	1.06	1.06	1.06	1.06	1.07	1.07	1.07	1.07	1.08
IFIXNRCOSTEXP85...	4.6	4.3	4.1	4.0	4.0	4.2	4.5	5.0	5.5	6.1	6.9	7.7	8.4	8.9	9.1	9.3
GNP72FERAW........	1176.4	1186.7	1196.0	1205.9	1214.4	1228.2	1235.9	1247.7	1257.9	1267.4	1279.9	1288.8	1292.9	1312.0	1309.9	1313.0
GNP72FE	1178.1	1186.7	1195.4	1204.3	1213.3	1222.8	1232.4	1242.3	1252.4	1262.6	1273.1	1283.6	1293.5	1304.0	1313.7	1322.5

	76:1	76:2	76:3	76:4	77:1	77:2	77:3	77:4	78:1	78:2	78:3	78:4	79:1	79:2	79:3	79:4
CORE	7.8	7.7	7.6	7.6	7.6	7.6	7.7	7.7	7.8	7.8	7.8	7.9	8.0	8.1	8.2	8.4
SHOCK...............	1.3	0.9	0.2	0.1	0.8	1.0	0.8	0.5	0.5	0.7	1.4	1.6	1.8	1.9	2.5	2.9
DEMAND	-2.7	-2.5	-2.4	-2.7	-2.5	-1.9	-1.8	-1.6	-1.7	-1.4	-1.2	-0.5	0.0	0.6	1.0	1.4
RCPIUYAMACRO	6.4	6.0	5.4	5.0	5.9	6.8	6.6	6.7	6.6	7.1	8.0	9.0	9.8	10.6	11.7	12.6
JAHEADJEAFE.......	1.68	1.71	1.74	1.77	1.81	1.84	1.88	1.91	1.95	1.98	2.02	2.06	2.10	2.14	2.19	2.23
JQ%MHNFFE79.......	1.08	1.09	1.09	1.09	1.10	1.10	1.10	1.11	1.11	1.11	1.11	1.12	1.12	1.12	1.13	1.13
IFIXNRCOSTEXP85...	9.5	9.6	9.7	9.8	9.9	9.9	10.0	10.1	10.2	10.3	10.4	10.4	10.4	10.4	10.4	10.4
GNP72FERAW........	1323.4	1331.8	1339.5	1349.6	1358.2	1370.7	1380.5	1392.3	1404.7	1417.6	1428.5	1441.0	1458.2	1463.0	1476.8	1487.6
GNP72FE	1331.5	1339.6	1347.7	1356.0	1364.4	1373.3	1382.5	1392.2	1402.3	1413.0	1424.0	1435.3	1447.4	1459.2	1471.1	1482.9

CORE is the core inflation rate,
SHOCK is the shock component of the inflation rate,
DEMAND is the demand component of core inflation,
RCPIUYAMACRO is the yearly change in the all-urban CPI as estimated from core, shock, and demand components,
JAHEADJEAFE is equilibrium wage gains,
JQ%MHNFFE79 is the productivity trend,
IFIXNRCOSTEXP85 is the smoothed yearly percentage change in the rental price of capital,
GNP72FERAW is nonsmoothed potential GNP,
GNP72FE is the full-employment level of real gross national product.

REFERENCES

Becker, Gary S. *Human Capital.* Washington: National Bureau of Economic Research, 1964.

Denison, Edward F. *Accounting for Slower Economic Growth.* Washington: Brookings Institution, 1979.

Denison, Edward F. *The Sources of Economic Growth in the United States and the Alternatives Before Us.* Supplementary Paper 13. New York: Committee for Economic Development, 1962.

Domar, Evsey. "Capital Expansion, Rate of Growth, and Employment." *Econometrica,* April 1946, pp. 137-147.

Dunlop, John T. *Wage Determination Under Trade Unions.* New York: Macmillan & Co., Ltd., 1944.

Eckstein, Otto. "Economic Theory and Econometric Models." Paper presented to the Ann Arbor Conference on Econometric Models, August 1978, to be published in the Conference volume.

Eckstein, Otto. *The Great Recession.* Amsterdam: North-Holland Publishing Co., 1978.

Eckstein, Otto and Brinner, Roger. "The Inflation Process in the United States." Study prepared for the Joint Economic Committee, February 22, 1972. Washington: U.S. Government Printing Office.

Eckstein, Otto and Girola, James. "Long-Term Properties of the Price-Wage Mechanism in the United States, 1891 to 1977." *Review of Economics and Statistics,* August 1978, pp. 323-333.

Eckstein, Otto and Wilson, Thomas A. "The Determination of Money Wages in American Industry." *The Quarterly Journal of Economics,* 76, August 1962, pp. 379-414.

Friedman, Milton. "The Role of Monetary Policy." *American Economic Review,* March 1968, pp. 1-17.

Frye, Jon and Gordon, Robert J. "The Variance and Acceleration of Inflation in the 1970's: Alternative Explanatory Models and Methods." NBER Working Paper No. 551, September 1980.

Gordon, Robert J. "The Impact of Aggregate Demand on Prices." Brookings Economic Papers, 1975:3, pp. 613-662.

Gordon, Robert J. "Can Econometric Policy Evaluation be Salvaged? A Comment," In *The Phillips Curve and Labor Markets,* edited by Karl Brunner and Allan H. Meltzer. Amsterdam: North-Holland Publishing Co., 1976, pp. 47-61.

Harrod, R.F. "Essay in Dynamic Theory." *Economic Journal,* 1939.

Kendrick, John W. *Productivity Trends in the United States.* Princeton: Princeton University Press, 1961.

Keynes, John Maynard. *The General Theory of Employment, Interest, and Money.* New York: Macmillan & Co., Ltd., 1936.

Leontief, Wassily W. *The Structure of American Economy, 1919-1939.* New York: Oxford University Press, 1941.

Lucas, R.E., Jr. "Econometric Policy Evaluation, A Critique." In *The Phillips Curve and Labor Markets,* edited by Karl Brunner and Allan H. Meltzer. Amsterdam: North-Holland Publishing Co., 1976, pp. 19-46.

Mill, John Stuart. *Principles of Political Economy.* London: 1848.

Modigliani, Franco and Papademos, Lucas. "Targets for Monetary Policy in the Coming Year." Brookings Economics Papers, 1975:1, pp. 141-163.

Mork, Knut Anton and Hall, Robert E. "Energy Prices, Inflation and Recession, 1974-75." *The Energy Journal,* July 1980, pp. 31-63.

Musgrave, Richard A. *The Theory of Public Finance.* New York: McGraw-Hill, Inc., 1959.

Muth, John F. "Rational Expectations and the Theory of Price Movements." *Econometrica,* July 1961, pp. 315-335.

Nordhaus, William D. "Recent Developments in Price Dynamics." In *The Econometrics of Price Determination,* edited by Otto Eckstein. Washington: Federal Reserve Board, 1972.

Norsworthy, J.R.; Harper, Michael J.; and Kunze, Kent. "The Slowdown in Productivity Growth." Brookings Economic Papers, 1979:2, pp. 387-421.

Okun, Arthur M. "Potential GNP: Its Measurement and Significance." In *Proceedings of the Economic Statistics Section of the American Statistical Association, Washington:* 1962.

Perloff, Jeffrey M. and Wachter, Michael. "A Production Function-Nonaccelerating Inflation Approach to Potential Output: Is Measured Potential Output Too High?" Carnegie-Rochester Conference Series, 10, 1979, *Three Aspects of Policy and Policy Making: Knowledge, Data and Institutions.* Edited by Karl Brunner and Allan H. Meltzer.

Sargent, Thomas J. "The Ends of Four Big Inflations." NBER Working Paper, October 1980.

Schultz, Theodore W. "Investment in Human Capital." *American Economic Review,* March 1961, pp. 1-17.

Siegel, Robin. "Why Has Productivity Slowed Down?" *Data Resources Review,* March 1979, pp. 59-65.

Smith, Adam. *Wealth of Nations.* 1776, Modern Library Edition. New York: Random House, 1937.

Solow, Robert M. "A Contribution to the Theory of Economic Growth." *Quarterly Journal of Economics,* February 1956, pp. 65-94.

Tobin, James. "The Wage-Price Mechanism: Overview of the Conference." In *The Econometrics of Price Determination,* edited by Otto Eckstein. Washington: Federal Reserve Board, 1972.

Wilson, Thomas A. "The Analysis of Machinery Prices." In *Study of Employment Growth and Price Levels.* Washington: Joint Economic Committee, 1959.

INDEX